MW00835246

CCNA
INTERVIEW QUESTIONS
YOU'LL MOST LIKELY BE ASKED

344
Interview Questions

VIBRANT
PUBLISHERS

CCNA
Interview Questions
You'll Most Likely Be Asked

ISBN-10: 1-946383-84-8
ISBN-13: 978-1-946383-84-6

Library of Congress Control Number: 2012900430

This publication is designed to provide accurate and authoritative information in regard to the subject matter covered. The author has made every effort in the preparation of this book to ensure the accuracy of the information. However, information in this book is sold without warranty either expressed or implied. The Author or the Publisher will not be liable for any damages caused or alleged to be caused either directly or indirectly by this book.

Vibrant Publishers books are available at special quantity discount for sales promotions, or for use in corporate training programs. For more information please write to **bulkorders@vibrantpublishers.com**

Please email feedback / corrections (technical, grammatical or spelling) to **spellerrors@vibrantpublishers.com**

To access the complete catalogue of Vibrant Publishers, visit **www.vibrantpublishers.com**

Table of Contents

Dear Reader,

Thank you for purchasing **CCNA Interview Questions You'll Most Likely Be Asked**. We are committed to publishing books that are content-rich, concise and approachable enabling more readers to read and make the fullest use of them. We hope this book provides the most enriching learning experience as you prepare for your interview.

Should you have any questions or suggestions, feel free to email us at **reachus@vibrantpublishers.com**

Thanks again for your purchase. Good luck with your interview!

- Vibrant Publishers Team

This page is intentionally left blank

CCNA Interview Questions

Review these typical interview questions and think about how you would answer them. Read the answers listed; you will find best possible answers along with strategies and suggestions.

This page is intentionally left blank

Chapter 1

TCP/IP and OSI Networking Models

1: What are the differences between TCP/IP and OCP Models?

Answer:

OSI or Open Systems Implementation is the theory and TCP/IP or Transmission Control Protocol/Internet Protocol is its implementation in practice. OSI comes with 7 layers while TCP/IP combines the top 3 layers of OSI and comes with 4 layers. The TCP/IP protocol was developed by the Department of Defence and is tangible. But the OSI model was developed by International Standards Organization and is not tangible.

2: Explain Broadcast, Multicast and Unicast.

Answer:

These are the different ways in which messages are sent in a network of computers. Unicast in networking means some message transmitted between two individual nodes in the network. There's only one sender and one receiver. Multicast means one sender sends a message to many nodes, though not all, in the network. In broadcast, one sender sends a message to all nodes in the network.

3: What is OSI reference model "network" layer?

Answer:

Network layer is layer 3 of the OSI reference model that defines logical addressing, routing and path determination. Examples of the protocols working at this layer are IP and IPX.

4: Which of the below are Transport layer protocols?

a) TCP

b) HTTP

c) IP

d) UDP

Answer:

a) TCP, d) HTTP

5: In networking terminology, what is "data encapsulation"?

Answer:

Data encapsulation is the process of putting headers and trailers around the data. Each layer encapsulates the upper layer's data into a new header and trailer. This process is repeated until reaching layer 1 which is responsible for transmitting the data over the transmission medium.

6: In which OSI reference model layer does HTTP operate?

  a) **Transport layer**

  b) **Network layer**

  c) **Application layer**

  d) **Physical layer**

Answer

c) Application layer

7: What is CSMA/CD and how does it work?

Answer:

When the data is transmitted by two or three nodes on a network through the cable, there occurs collision. So, CSMA/CA (Carrier Sense Multiple Access/ Collision Avoidance) is used. Before transmitting the data on the cable, NIC (network Interface Card) checks the cable if any transmission is going on; if no, it sends the data or waits for the transmission to finish.

If two NIC senses the medium at the same time and send the data, there occurs collision. Then the node detects the collision and sends a 'Jam Signal' to all other nodes on that network.

8: What are the two kinds of transport possible and give some example?

Answer:

  a) Reliable and unreliable are the two kinds of transport

possible

b) The transport varies according to the application

c) The reliable protocol is defined by TCP

d) The unreliable protocol is defined by UDP

e) Example:

UDP is used in SNMP

TCP is used in HTTP

9: How TCP ensures a reliable as well as controlled transport?

Answer:

a) The reliable transport is ensured by the assurance of data delivery

b) The controlled transport is ensured by congestion control which means when the resources are busy it does not send the data

10: For an inherent requirement application which protocol would be better to use at the transport layer?

Answer:

TCP protocol would be better to use because it resends the acknowledgement when the packet is not received

11: When the client will declare that the server is unreachable if the client sends data to a server?

Answer:

a) Even though the server does not send an acknowledgement, the client will not declare the server that it is unreachable.

Instead, it resends the data packet until it reaches its threshold value. Declares that the server is unreachable

b) If the client does not receive any acknowledgment after reaching its threshold value, then it declares that the server is unreachable

12: Why the windowing concept is introduced in TCP?

Answer:

In TCP, an acknowledgement is sent every time when a fragment of data is received. This increases the traffic when a large amount of data is sent. To avoid this, the windowing concept is introduced.

13: List the TCP/IP port for following:

a) **FTP**

b) **TELNET**

c) **HTTP**

d) **SNMP**

e) **POP3**

Answer:

a) FTP-21

b) TELNET-23

c) HTTP-80

d) SNMP-25

e) POP3-110

14: What are the advantages of UDP over TCP?

Answer:

a) Both are transport layer protocols.UDP is a connectionless protocol while TCP is a connection-oriented protocol.

b) UDP provides low overhead data delivery than TCP

c) UDP find applications in the Domain Name System (DNS), Video Streaming, Voice over IP (VoIP) whereas TCP has applications in Web Browsers, E-mail, File Transfers

Chapter **2**

LAN Fundamentals

15: Explain the Token Ring Operation.

Answer:

In a Token Ring network, the stations are arranged in a ring topology. Empty tokens that are circulated in the network are captured to send messages by the station. There's a control token that contains the details regarding the destination and the data. This token is passed on in the network until it reaches the intended destination. Different stations pass the token on to the connected neighboring rings until it reaches the destination. More information is added to the token by altering the T bit. Finally, when the destination station receives the message, it sets the token bit to 0 which then reaches the sender through the network. When the sender receives the 0 token it confirms that the message has reached the intended destination.

16: Explain FDDI

Answer:

FDDI is Fiber Distributed Data Interface, developed by the ANSI to define a dual token ring network that carries data at a speed of 100+ Mbps through a Fiber medium which renders it faster and safer. For smaller networks covering shorter distances, the CDDI using Copper can be implemented successfully. But for larger networks covering larger area, more expensive Fiber Optics cable needs to be used which provides faster and more reliable data transmission.

17: Which connector type is used in Ethernet cables?

   a) RJ11

   b) RJ12

   c) RJ55

   d) RJ45

Answer:

d) RJ45

18: What is broadcast MAC address and what is its value?

Answer:

The broadcast MAC address is a type of layer 2 address that is used to deliver data to all devices in the same broadcast domain of the sender. The source sends only one frame on the network and the switch replicates it to all ports in the same broadcast domain of the source. The broadcast MAC address has a value of FFFF.FFFF.FFFF.

19: Describe "twisted" pair cables and mention why they are twisted.

Answer:

Ethernet cables contain 8 wires in 4 pairs groups. Each pair is twisted so that the magnetic field created by one wire cancels out the magnetic field created by the other wire. This enhances performance and decreases transmission noise.

20: Describe how you can make an Ethernet cross-over cable.

Answer:

Ethernet cross-over cable is created by connecting Pins 1 and 2 on one side of the cable to pins 3 and 6 on the other side. The other pins' connectivity doesn't matter as the network device uses only 4 wires of the 8 to send and receive data.

21: What typical cable type do you use to connect two switches together?

   a) **Straight-through cable**

   b) **Roll-over cable**

   c) **Console cable**

   d) **Cross-over cable**

Answer:

d) Cross-over cable

22: What is the maximum cable length in Fast Ethernet (IEEE 802.3u) standard?

   a) 100m

   b) 200m

   c) 50m

   d) 500m

Answer:

a) 100m

Chapter 3

WAN Fundamentals

23: What are these devices used for in a WAN network - Access Server, Modem and WAN Switch?

Answer:

The WAN network functions with the help of Modem, Access Server, WAN Switch, Digital Service Unit and an ISDN terminal. The model converts digital signals to analog at the sending point and the analog signals to digital at the receiving point. The WAN switch connects one network point to many for interworking. It enables bandwidth sharing among the various services, helps recovery from network outages, and also helps the network design and management. The access server connects and controls the dial-in and dial-out connections.

24: What is ISDN?

Answer:

ISDN stands for Integrated Services Digital Network which is widely used in the switched Telephone network used by the public. The ISDN protocol allows the network to digitally transmit voice, data and videos within a network and to other networks that connect with it. ISDN allows circuit-switched and packet-switched transmissions. This technology is widely being used in the telephone network and broadcast industry. ISDN is the heart and soul for cable-broadband industry.

25: What are the advantages of the Layered model in networking?

Answer:

The layered networking model provides a lot of flexibility to the implementers. You can change a particular layer to customize it without affecting the other layers. You can work on different layers individually for specific processes or applications without affecting the others. This ensures that all required specialization is possible to make your network more reliable and functional for your organization. Layering also lets you troubleshoot more efficiently.

26: What is the speed of E1 line?
   a) 64 kbps
   b) 1.544 Mbps
   c) 2.048 Mbps
   d) 1.026 Mbps
Answer:

c) 2.048 Mbps

27: Which of the below are OSI layer2 WAN protocols?

a) HDLC

b) PPP

c) Frame-relay

d) Ethernet

Answer:

a) HDLC, b) PPP, c) Frame-relay

28: Which of the below are types of Digital Subscriber line (DSL)?

a) ADSL

b) HDSL

c) VDSL

d) NDSL

Answer:

a) ADSL, b) HDSL, c) VDSL

29: When connecting to internet, which of the below remote access technologies are considered always on?

a) ADSL

b) Cable Modems

c) Analog modems

d) HDSL

Answer:

a) ADS, b) Cable Modems, d) HDSL

30: You use a DSL connection at home for internet connectivity. You use an IP address of 10.10.10.10 on your PC. The DSL is doing NAT for your IP to 41.111.23.23 to access internet. According to NAT terminology, what is the name of your IP address after being NATed to the public IP as viewed on internet?

a) Inside local

b) Inside global

c) Outside local

d) Outside global

Answer:

b) Inside global

31: Which protocols below are layer2 protocols that can be used over WAN?

a) PPP

b) OSPF

c) HDLC

d) EIGRP

Answer:

a) PPP, c) HDLC

32: Which command below do you use to configure PPP on a serial interface?

a) use ppp

b) set ppp

c) encapsulation ppp

d) protocol ppp

Answer:

c) encapsulation ppp

33: When configuring Internet Access Router in small office, which features below are usually configured to allow internet access for users?

    a) **PAT**

    b) **BGP**

    c) **DHCP**

    d) **Telnet**

Answer

a) PAT, c) DHCP

34: Why PAT is used when configuring SOHO routers?

Answer:

PAT (Port Address Translation) is a NAT type in which each computer on LAN is translated to the same IP address, but with a different port number assignment. Small Office/Home Office (SOHO) routers are used in small offices to connect users to internet. It uses one Public IP address for internet access. So PAT is used to translate users' IP addresses to this public IP.

This page is intentionally left blank

Chapter **4**

IP Addressing and Routing

35: What are the metrics considered in Routing goals?

Answer:

Routing algorithms use certain measures and metrics to find out the most efficient network route involving minimal cost. These involve the following:

a) **Reliability** – Reliability measures how reliable the network is. It is the bit-error rate in a network. Since some paths have more errors than others and some links can be repaired faster, reliability measure is important.

b) **Path Length** – This measure either the cost related to each hop or the number of hops required for a message to reach the destination from the host.

c) **Bandwidth** – Bandwidth measures the volume of data that can be transmitted through the network.

d) **Delay** – It is the time taken for the message to reach the destination from the source. The bandwidth, network congestion, queue, distance etc contribute to the delay.

e) **Communication Cost** – This is the cost of maintaining the network of communication.

f) **Load** – Determines the volume of data being handled by the router in a network.

36: Explain Static versus Dynamic Routing.

Answer:

Static routing is done manually. The Administrator will assign a static address to the router which will identify it. This address will remain static till it is changed manually, or the router is reset. The problem with static routing is that, if any change is there in the network path, the route has to be manually altered. Otherwise the network may not work. In dynamic routing, whenever the network connection is established, the best available route is determined based on the available network. This involves some overheads in determining the route. But dynamic routing is preferred when you do not have to access a particular station exclusively.

37: Describe the routing process on the router from the point a packet enters one interface till it exits from another one.

Answer:

The router checks the destination IP of the packet then it tries to find a match for the destination in its routing table. If a match is found the router gets the next hop IP from the routing table along with the outgoing interface. It then sends an ARP request to get the MAC address of the next hop. It encapsulates the packet into a frame with the router's MAC address as the source MAC and the next hop MAC address as the destination MAC. Then the router sends the frame out of the outgoing interface.

38: Which of the below are class B network addresses?

    a) **192.168.1.40**

    b) **190.19.22.32**

    c) **130.17.18.20**

    d) **10.16.11.190**

Answer

b) 190.19.22.32, c) 130.17.18.20

39: What are the default IP address classes? What are their ranges?

Answer:

The three default network classes are called A, B, and C

Class A: 1.0.0.0 to 126.0.0.0

Class B: 128.0.0.0 to 191.255.0.0

Class C: 192.0.0.0 to 223.255.255.0

40: What is a routing protocol?

Answer:

The routing protocol lets the routers in a network communicate with each other to pass on the information on routing and other messages and updates. This helps the routers to choose the best route between two nodes in a network to transmit the information. The route is chosen with the help of routing algorithms.

41: Describe "classless" addressing.

Answer:

Classless addressing is an addressing method in which the routing process considers the network and subnet parts of the address together without the rules of Class A, B, and C addressing. This addressing system calls for eliminating the notion of address classes entirely, creating a classless addressing scheme allowing the subnet boundary to move to the right, into the network portion. This mandates sending the subnet mask in the routing updates between the routers.

42: A router received a packet on one of its interfaces. It searched its routing table for a match and found a route pointing out of its Fast Ethernet interface into another router. Which protocol will the router use to know the address that will be placed in the layer2 frame?

   a) DNS

   b) RARP

   c) ARP

   d) RIP

Answer

c) ARP

43: Describe IP routing protocols mentioning three functions of them.

Answer:

The routing protocols are responsible for exchanging routing updates between routers. Routing protocols' functions include:

a) Dynamically learn and fill the routing table with a route to all subnets in the network

b) When multiple routes are learned for a network, select the best route or load balance the traffic over them

c) Notice when routes in the table are no longer valid, and remove them from the routing table

d) Prevent routing loops

44: This IP address 143.111.232.022 belongs to which address class?

Answer:

Since the beginning of the IP address falls between 128 to 191. This IP address belongs to address class B.

45: Write the network address of this IP address 193.123.112.023 and also identify its class.

Answer:

a) The network address of the given IP address is 193.123.112.0

b) And the IP's range falls between 192 to 223, hence it comes under the 'class C'

46: What are the steps involved in computing 'Address Assignment'?

Answer:

Following calculations should takes place in the same order:

a) Broadcast Address

b) Lowest Host Address

c) Host Address Range

d) Network Address

e) Highest Host Address

47: How address is dynamically assigned to host?

Answer:

Using the DHCP method, IP addresses can be automatically assigned to a host. It does not need to be manually updated. DHCP uses the address pool to assign address to the client. Also assigned address can be reused if the host is powered down or taken out of the network. This feature is favored for mobile users.

Chapter **5**

TCP/IP Applications

48: Explain the following:

  a) **PPP**
  b) **SNTP**
  c) **VPN**

Answer:

PPP or Point to Point Protocol is used when you need to transmit information through serial lines. This protocol is widely used by the Internet Service Providers or ISPs to enable individual computers connect to a network or the internet.

SNTP or Simple Network Time Protocol is used for time management in network. This is widely used in network identification and authentication which needs to be time-bound.

VPN or Virtual Private Network lets you connect privately to an external machine over a public network without compromising the security.

49: Explain UDP

Answer:

UDP or User Datagram Protocol is a fast but unreliable protocol which cannot be used with all applications or networks. It renders much faster because there's no installation required. It is like a plug and play concept. It is unreliable since there's no error checking, or even checking whether the message sent was received properly by the receiver. It assumes that the sender will resend the message if it does not get any response over a time period. There are no checksums either. UDP works well for audio and video broadcasts where the data needs to be delivered fast but there's no need to cross-check its delivery.

50: Which protocol below allows network hosts to resolve network IPs of other hosts knowing their hostnames?

   a) DHCP

   b) DNS

   c) OSPF

   d) ARP

Answer:

b) DNS

51: What is TCP Error Recovery?

Answer:

TCP error recovery serves in detecting transmission errors and recovering them. Using Sequence Number field in one direction combined with the Acknowledgment field in the opposite direction, it detects and retransmits packets with errors.

52: Which of the below are functions of TCP protocol?

  a) Error recovery

  b) Encryption

  c) Flow control using windowing

  d) NAT

Answer:

a) Error recovery, c) Flow control using windowing

53: Which of the below protocols use TCP as their transport protocol?

  a) SNMP

  b) HTTP

  c) FTP

  d) IP

Answer:

b) HTTP, c) FTP

54: Describe TCP connection establishment and termination processes.

Answer:

TCP is a connection-oriented protocol. To establish a connection, TCP performs three-way handshaking in which the source sends a SYN packet, the destination sends a SYN/ACK packet and then the source sends ACK packet.TCP terminates connections using the four-way termination sequence using the FIN and ACK flags in which the source sends FIN/ACK packet, the destinations replies with ACK packet, the destination sends FIN/ACK packet and then the source replies with ACK packet.

55: Why UDP is suitable for VOIP traffic?

Answer:

Voice data is extremely sensitive to time and greatly benefits from the fast transportation which is associated with the UDP because its headers don't have any kind of reliability and for practical purposes do not require a guarantee that data is transmitted which enhances usage and speed of VOIP. Hence UDP is suited for VOIP traffic.

Chapter 6

Network Security

56: Explain ARP and RARP

Answer:

ARP is Address Resolution Protocol and as the name suggests, it helps to map the network address to the hardware of a particular computer in the network. It works between the data link layer and the network layer in the OSI model to resolve the address. RARP is the Reverse Address Resolution Protocol and does just the opposite of ARP wherein the machine requests for its IP address from the network gateway router. The IP address corresponding to the MAC (Media Access Control) address is accessed by the RARP to store in the machine for using later when required. It can be used in FDDI, Token ring and Ethernet networks.

57: What is SSO?

Answer:

SSO stands for Single Sign On authentication. A session or cookie is used to store the user authentication details so that the user gets access to the related services without having to maintain a separate user id/password combination for each related service. Google's authentication can be considered as an example of SSO since a single login can give you access to most of Google's services such as the Google Drive, Google+, Gmail, Google Photos etc.

58: What is the DoS attack?

Answer:

Denial of service (DoS) attacks flood the network with packets to make the network unusable, preventing any useful communication with the network's users and servers.

59: What is Spyware?

Answer:

A spyware is a virus that looks for private or sensitive information, tracking what the user does with the computer, and passing the information back to the attacker in the Internet.

60: What are Firewalls and what is their function?

Answer:

Firewalls are a security feature that checks all data passing through the network. It checks every packet received and sent and filters unwanted traffic. Since every packet will have the sender and receiver information, the firewall will check those and determine whether it is genuine or spam data. The packets usually have the TCP & UDP port numbers and the source IP address.

61: Describe the DMZ network zone highlighting its functionality.

Answer:

As some hosts in the Enterprise need to be accessible from the Internet, the firewall has an interface connected to another small part of the Enterprise network, called the Demilitarized zone (DMZ). The DMZ is a place to put devices that need to be accessible from Internet, but that access puts them at higher risk. So, they are separated from network Internal hosts.

This page is intentionally left blank

Chapter **7**

LAN Switching Concepts

62: What are HUB, Switch, and Router?

Answer:

The Hub operates in the Physical Layer of a network, allowing hosts to communicate with each other without bothering about what information is being passed on. It is a device that lets hosts connect to each other. When it receives a packet, it broadcasts it to all the hosts connected. The Switch also lets hosts communicate with each other like a Hub, but it ensures that the packet is sent only to the intended hosts. The Switch is more intelligent as it reads the data and determines the hosts. It works at the Data-link layer and makes the network more efficient by saving the bandwidth. The Router works at the Network layer and transmits the data outside the intranet or local network. While the Hub and Switch work within a local network, the Router connects you to the external network.

63: How does the switch understand the MAC address?

Answer:

When the frames are transmitted over the network, the Switch will closely review the MAC address of the source and compares it with the table it already has in its memory. If the MAC address is not available in the address table, it adds the same along with the port number where the frame was received. If the MAC address is already available in the address table of the Switch, it will compare the ports and update any changes in the port.

64: Which field in the frame does the switch use to deliver the frame to its destination?

   a) Source MAC address

   b) FCS filed

   c) Destination MAC address

   d) Destination IP address

Answer:

c) Destination MAC address

65: Describe the process of building the switch's MAC address table.

Answer:

When the switch receives a frame, it looks into the source MAC address inside it. If it is not already in the Mac address table, it adds a new entry for this MAC with the corresponding interface being the one that received this frame. This is the process of building the switch's MAC address table.

66: The frames of the set of LAN interfaces collide with each other, however not with frames sent by any other devices in the network is called

   a) Broadcast domain

   b) Collision domain

   c) VLAN

   d) User domain

Answer

b) Collision domain

67: What is STP?

Answer:

Spanning Tree Protocol (STP) is a layer 2 protocol that is responsible for avoiding layer 2 loops by exchanging messages between switches to keep each switch aware of the topology and avoid loops. STP is a vital component of every layer 2 network.

68: How do you define a VLAN?

Answer:

VLAN or Virtual LAN lets you connect computers from the external network with your LAN to function as if they are in the same local network. This is done using high-end switches. VLANs make the network scalable and secure while also allowing broadcasts and multicasts to be shared. VLANs make server relocations almost invisible to the local network. They make the network more flexible and easily manageable. The major risks involved with VLANs are that they are more susceptible to virus attacks and may require high-end routers in a larger network.

69: What is the maximum segment length of Ethernet CAT5 UTP cable?

a) 200m

b) 10m

c) 1km

d) 100m

Answer:

d) 100m

Chapter 8

Cisco LAN Switches Operation and Configuration

70: Which cable type do you use to access the console of Cisco switch?

Answer:

To access the switch's console user must use a roll-over cable in which pins 1 through 8 in one end are crossly connected to pins 8 through 1 in the other end.

71: You want to save the router configuration. Which command do you use to accomplish that?

   a)   Router#save configuration

b) Router#copy running-config startup-config

c) Router#save all configuration

d) Router#copy all configuration to flash

Answer:

b) Router#copy running-config startup-config

72: Why is it recommended to use SSH instead of telnet in accessing Cisco devices?

Answer:

Secure Shell (SSH) is a network protocol for secure data communication that uses encryption to secure the communication between the remote management PC and Cisco devices. While SSH uses encryption, Telnet sends data as clear text, so it is unsecure. So, for better security, it is recommended to use SSH instead of Telnet.

73: You want to configure Telnet password of "cisco" for Cisco switch. Which command below do you use?

a) Switch(config)#telnet password cisco

b) Switch(config-line)#password cisco

c) Switch(config)#remote password cisco

d) Switch(config-line)#telnet password cisco

Answer:

b) Switch(config-line)#password cisco

74: In which mode can the network administrator configure enable password for the router?

a) User mode

b) Privileged mode

c) Global configuration mode

d) Interface configuration mode

Answer:

c) Global configuration mode.

75: How do you reach the global configuration mode of Cisco switch remotely using your PC?

Answer:

You need to telnet or SSH to the router using a hyper terminal program, authenticate your credential with the switch, enter privileged mode using "enable" command and then enter the global configuration mode using "config terminal" command.

76: To reach enable mode from a vty (Telnet or SSH), the switch must be configured with:

a) An IP address

b) Login security on the vty lines

c) An enable password

d) An ACL on interfaces

Answer:

a) An IP address, b) Login security on the vty lines, c) An enable password

77: How do you enable SSH access to the router?

Answer:

Configure domain name on the router using "ip domain-name" command, create SSH key pair using "crypto key" command, configure username and password using "username name password pass" command and configure the router to use usernames locally by "login local" command or on AAA server by using "aaa new-model" command.

78: Which command do you use to configure a gateway of 10.10.10.1 for a switch?

a) Switch(config)#ip route 0.0.0.0 0.0.0.0

b) Switch(config)#ip default-gateway 10.10.10.1

c) Switch(config)#gateway 10.10.10.1

d) Switch(config)#ip gateway 10.10.10.1

Answer:

b) Switch(config)#ip default-gateway 10.10.10.1

79: What is "port security"?

Answer:

Port security is a security feature in which the administrator restricts access to switch interfaces by client's MAC address so that only the authorized devices can access it.

80: Which command do you use to configure a new VLAN on a switch?

a) Switch(config)# vlan "vlan-id"

b) Switch(config)#create vlan "vlan-id"

c) Switch(config)#add vlan "vlan-id"

d) Switch(config)#new vlan "vlan-id"

Answer:

a) Switch(config)# vlan "vlan-id"

81: How do you view the configured VLANs on a switch?

a) Switch#display vlan

b) Switch#show all vlan

c) Switch#debug vlan

d) Switch#show vlan brief

Answer:

d) Switch#show vlan brief

82: What is CDP?

Answer:

CDP stands for Cisco Discovery Protocol

a) The information about the neighboring switches and routers can be determined using the 'Cisco Discovery Protocol'

b) This can be done by without knowing the password of the neighboring devices

c) The information discovered are IOS version, IP address, directly connected neighbor's interface, device type and model, and hostname

83: You issued a "shutdown" command under one interface of a switch. Which of the below is the correct status of the interface?

a) Line status is "up" and protocol status is "down"

b) Line status is "down" and protocol status is "down"

c) Line status is "administratively down" and protocol status is "down"

d) Line status is "down" and protocol status is "up"

Answer:

c) Line status is "administratively down" and protocol status is "down"

84: How do you view the stored MAC addresses on a switch?

a) Switch#show mac addresses

b) Switch#show mac address-table

c) Switch#show all addresses

d) Switch#debug mac address

Answer:

b) Switch#show mac address-table.

Chapter **9**

Wireless LAN Concepts

85: Describe WLAN Infrastructure mode.

Answer:

WLAN Infrastructure mode is a design in which each wireless device communicates with an Access Point (AP), with the AP connecting the wireless LAN to the network infrastructure using wired Ethernet cable connected to a switch.

86: Which of the below are security standards used in WLANs?

a) WEP

b) WNA

c) SSID.

d) WPA2

Answer:

a) WEP, d) WPA2

87: What is the maximum speed of 802.11a WLAN standard?

a) 11 Mbps

b) 55 Mbps

c) 54 Mbps

d) 45Mbps

Answer

c) 54 Mbps

88: Which of the below is a private class B IP address?

a) 10.199.23.22

b) 130.23.11.129

c) 41.23.212.32

d) 172.18.23.11

Answer

d) 172.18.23.11

Chapter 10

IP Addressing and Subnetting

89: What is a private IP address?

Answer:

A private IP address is an IP address that is un-routed over internet and can be used internally in the network. Private IP addresses are in the ranges:

  a) 10.0.0.0 through 10.255.255.255

  b) 172.16.0.0 through 172.31.255.255

  c) 192.168.0.0 through 192.168.255.255

90: If the subnet mask 255.255.255.192 is used with a class C network, how many subnets and how many users per subnet could exist?

a)   2 subnets with 62 users in each subnet

b)   4 subnets with 62 users in each subnet

c)   8 subnets with 32 users in each subnet

d)   4 subnets with 32 users in each subnet

Answer

b) 4 subnets with 62 users in each subnet

91: What is the broadcast IP address of the network 192.168.14.32/28?

a)   192.168.14.62

b)   192.168.14.46

c)   192.168.14.30

d)   192.168.14.255

Answer:

b) 192.168.14.46

92: You have a class C network that you will use inside your network. What subnet mask can you use to get at least 6 subnets with 5 users in each one? Your design should allow for maximum number of subnets for future expansion.

a)   255.255.255.248

b)   255.255.255.0

c)   255.255.255.240

d)   255.255.255.224

Answer:

a) 255.255.255.248

93: Which of the below IP addresses are in the same subnet with the IP address 190.22.34.123 with mask 255.255.255.0?

a) 190.22.34.4

b) 190.22.34.53

c) 190.22.33.24

d) 190.22.11.23

Answer:

a) 190.22.34.4, b) 190.22.34.53

94: Which address does the router use to forward the traffic?

a) The source IP address

b) The destination IP address

c) The source MAC address

d) The destination MAC address

Answer

b) The destination IP address

This page is intentionally left blank

Chapter 11

Cisco Routers Operation and Configuration

95: What are Cisco SOHO routers?

Answer:

Small Office / Home Office (SOHO) routers are small, low cost routers that usually serve users in very small business. These routers connect users to internet using high-speed internet access service such as ADSL.

96: Which cable type do you use to connect a router to a switch?

Answer:

"Straight-through cable" in which pins 1 through 8 in one end connect to pins 1 through 8 in the other end is used to connect a router to a switch.

97: You want to view all IP addresses that are configured on all interfaces of a Cisco router. Which command below will you use?

a) Show configured ip

b) Show all ip addresses

c) Show ip

d) Show ip interface brief

Answer

d) Show ip interface brief

98: How do you troubleshoot an interface with "administratively down -down" status?

Answer:

An interface in "administratively down -down" status means that this interface is disabled using the command "shutdown". To enable the interface back you can use the command "no shutdown".

99: What command below will you use to configure the ip address 10.10.10.10/24 on a router interface?

a) ip address 10.10.10.10 255.0.0.0

b) ip 10.10.10.10 255.255.255.0

c) use ip 10.10.10.10

d) ip address 10.10.10.10 255.255.255.0

Answer:

d) ip address 10.10.10.10 255.255.255.0

Chapter **12**

Routing Protocols Concepts and Troubleshooting

100: What is the route metric?

Answer:

Route metric is a numeric value representing the "goodness" of each route. This value is used by routing algorithms to determine whether one route would perform better than another. Route metric examples are hop-count in RIP protocol and Cost in OSPF.

101: A router has two routes with different metrics. How will the router deal with them?

   a) The router always uses the route with the highest metric

   b) The router always uses the route with the lowest metric

   c) The router will load balance the traffic using the two

routes

d) The metric doesn't affect the route selection

Answer:

b) The router always uses the route with the lowest metric

102: What is the RIP metric?

Answer:

Routing Information Protocol (RIP) uses a metric called hop-count which is the number of routers in the path to the destination network. The maximum value for hop-count is 16 which indicates that the network defined in the update is unreachable.

103: Which parameters does EIGRP use to calculate its metric?

Answer:

Enhanced Interior Gateway Routing Protocol (EIGRP) can use Delay, Bandwidth, Reliability and Load to calculate its metric. By default, Cisco routers use only bandwidth and delay in the metric formula.

104: Which routing protocols below support VLSM?

a) RIP

b) EIGRP

c) OSPF

d) RIPv2

Answer:

b) EIGRP, c) OSPF, d) RIPv2

105: A router has two routes to the same destination; one learned by OSPF and the other learned by EIGRP. Which route will be used and why?

Answer:

EIGRP has administrative distance of 90 while OSPF has administrative distance of 110. So EIGRP route will be used because it has lower administrative distance.

106: What is the function of ARP protocol?

Answer:

The function of ARP protocol is:

a) To get the physical address, the host generates the ARP request and broadcast that onto the network

b) The IP address of the host will be in the ARP request

c) The host that contains the broadcasted IP address, replies to the requested the host with its physical address

107: You want to display detailed network configuration on Windows based host. This should include all interfaces, including IP address, mask, default gateway, and DNS IP addresses. Which command below should you use?

a) ipconfig /all

b) show ip address

c) show configuration

d) list network configuration

Answer

a) ipconfig /all

108: What command do you use on Cisco router to view the routing table?

   a)   show routing table

   b)   view routing table

   c)   show routing information

   d)   show ip route

Answer:

d) show ip route

109: What are the steps needed to enable telnet access to a router?

Answer:

In order to enable telnet access to a router you must perform the below steps:

   a)   Configure telnet password under line vty using "password" command

   b)   Configure "login" command under line vty

110: Which command below will check reachability between two end points by listing the IP addresses of the routers in the route?

   a)   ping

   b)   traceroute

   c)   reach

   d)   telnet

Answer:

b) traceroute

111: What is a routed protocol?

Answer:

Routed protocols are the data being transported across the networks. These protocols define a packet structure and logical addressing allowing routers to forward packets. An example of routed protocols is Internet Protocol (IP).

112: Which of the below is a routed protocol?

a) RIP

b) OSPF

c) EIGRP

d) IPX

Answer:

d) IPX

113: Which of the below are routing protocols?

a) IP

b) RIPv1

c) IPX

d) RIPv2

Answer:

b) RIPv1, d) RIPv2.

114: What is an IGP?

Answer:

Interior Gateway Protocol (IGP) is a routing protocol that was intended to be used inside a single Autonomous system (AS). An autonomous system is a single routing domain, or network, controlled by one individual or organization. Examples of IGP protocols are RIP, OSPF and EIGRP.

115: What is the metric used in distance vector routing protocols?

Answer:

Distance vector routing protocols use hop-count as a metric which is the number of routers in the path from the source to the destination. The maximum metric value is 16 which indicates an unreachable destination.

116: Which routing protocol below is a hybrid routing protocol?

   a) OSPF

   b) EIGRP

   c) IGRP

   d) RIPv2

Answer:

b) EIGRP

117: What is routing convergence?

Answer:

Routing convergence is part of the routing table update process. When a link fails or changes, updates are sent across the network that describe changes in the network topology. When convergence occurs, all routers have the same topological information for the network.

118: Which routing protocol below doesn't send subnet mask in the routing updates?

   a) OSPF

   b) RIPv2

   c) EIGRP

   d) RIPv1

Answer:

d) RIPv1

119: Which routing protocol below supports unequal-cost load balancing?

   a) OSPF

   b) RIPv1

   c) RIPv2

   d) EIGRP

Answer

d) EIGRP

120: What is the administrative distance of OSPF?

   a) 110

   b) 120

   c) 90

   d) 10

Answer

a) 110

121: What is Route poisoning?

Answer:

Route poisoning is a mechanism used by distance vector routing protocol in which the routers advertise a route, but with a special metric value called infinity to indicate that this route has failed. This decreases routing protocol convergence time and avoids routing loops.

122: Describe Split Horizon.

Answer:

Split horizon is a method used by distance vector routing protocols to prevent routing loops in a network. According to Split Horizon rule, a router never advertises a route out of the interface through which it learned it.

123: Compare Link State routing protocols to Distance Vector routing protocols.

Answer:

Link state routing protocols can be compared to Distance vector routing protocols as follows:

a) In Link State, all routers learn the same detailed information about all routers and subnets in the network while they don't in Distance Vector

b) Link state protocols depend on more accurate path parameters when calculating the metric. While distance vector protocols depend only on hop count

c) Link State protocols have faster convergence than Distance Vector protocols

124: Which routing protocol uses the link state logic?

a) RIPv1

b) RIPv2

c) OSPF

d) EIGRP

Answer:

c) OSPF

125: You issued "show ip route" command on a Cisco router. Which letter below will appear in the start of the EIGRP learned route?

a) O

b) S

c) E

d) D

Answer:

d) D

126: What does the "passive-interface" command do in EIGRP?

Answer:

"Passive-interface" command in EIGRP prevents the router from establishing EIGRP neighbor relationship with neighbor routers on that interface. It also stops both sending and receiving outgoing and incoming EIGRP routing updates respectively on that interface.

127: Which command below would you use to show only OSPF learned routes in the routing table?

   a) show ip ospf
   b) show ip route ospf
   c) show ospf routes
   d) show only ospf

Answer:

b) show ip route ospf

128: In troubleshooting OSPF problems, which command can you use to show the neighbor of OSPF enabled router?

   a) show adjacency
   b) show neighbors
   c) show ip ospf neighbor
   d) show ospf adjacent

Answer:

c) show ip ospf neighbor

Routing Protocols

129: What is the 'routing protocol' and 'routed protocol'?

Answer:

Routing protocol is used to route the data packets from source to destination through the network.

Routed protocol is the data packets that get transferred between source and destination using routing protocol.

130: What is the purpose of a metric?

Answer:

A metric is used to estimate the best path among the available paths to reach the destination. Metric is the value calculated by a routing protocol in each possible path. Each routing protocol has different metrics. The path with the lower metric value is low of cost and is preferred to reach the destination.

131: Name some routing protocols and routed protocols.

Answer:

Routing Protocol:

a) **BGP:** Border Gateway Protocol

b) **NLSP:** Netware Link Service Protocol

c) **RTMP:** Real Time Messaging Protocol

Routed Protocol:

a) Apple-talk

b) IP

c) IPX

132: Describe about IP routing.

Answer:

a) The packets are sent to the destination using routing. The internet uses 'Hop by Hop' method to transfer the data

b) When the packet is sent to the next hop, there the destination address is examined, and best next hop is determined

c) The packet is sent to the best next hop and the same process continues till it reaches the destination

d) The logical address i.e.) IP address remains the same whereas the MAC address (hardware interface address) changes with each hop

133: How Distance vector protocol differs from link state vector protocol?

Answer:

a) Distance vector protocol sends the entire routing table to the nearest neighbor at regular interval

b) Whereas the link state routing protocol sends the routing changes to all other routers in that area

134: In the given diagram which routing path will be taken by using RIPv1 and why?

Answer:

The above diagram takes the following routing path source, L1, L2, Destination. Because the hop count of this path is 2 which is lesser than the other path (hop count =3).

135: List Classless and Classfull routing protocol.

Answer:

a) Classless routing protocol:

RIPv2,

EIGRP,

OSPF,

IS-IS,

BGP

b) Classful routing protocol:

RIPv1 and

IGRP

136: Identify the metric used by distance vector protocol.

Answer:

a) bandwidth

b) delay

c) cost

d) hop count

137: What are the disadvantages of proxy ARP?

Answer:

The disadvantages of proxy ARP are:

a) It increases the ARP traffic

b) It cannot be used for all network topologies

c) It does not work with networks that don't use ARP for address resolution

138: What is ARP spoofing?

Answer:

ARP spoofing is a technique used by attacker to insert the wrong MAC address into a network by sending fake ARP messages. By this frame can be sent to the wrong destination. This pay way to other attacks such as such as denial of service, man in the middle, or session hijacking

139: In which MAC method of sharing there is no collision?

Answer:

The method of sharing is Controlled access method because it allows only one station to transmit at a time. Each station must wait for their own turn examples include token passing, FDDI. Though there is no collision it is inefficient as it causes much delay this method is also called as scheduled or deterministic method

140: Describe about FTP and TFTP protocols.

Answer:

a) Both the protocols are used for the application layer

b) TFTP (Trivial File Transfer Protocol):

    i) Allows only to send and receive files

    ii) Provides no authentication and security

c) FTP (File Transfer Protocol):

    i) Provides access to directories and files

    ii) Allows to change the file contents, copy the files and transfers the files between the system on the network

141: How will you set the bandwidth usage of EIGRP?

Answer:

a) EIGRP uses only the 50% percent of the available bandwidth. To change the default range,

   ip bw-prc eigrp number percent

b) To use the default bandwidth,

   no ip bw-prc eigrp number percent

bw - bandwidth

prc - percent

number - system number

percent - required bandwidth percentage

142: What is the formula to compute the waiting time of the queued packet before transmitting?

Answer:

The formula to compute the waiting time is:

Waiting time = (8*100* pkts_size)/(bw *bw_perc)

pkts_size - packet Size(bytes)

bw - Bandwidth(kbps)

bw_perc - Bandwidth percentage

RIP Routing protocol

143: Which is routing protocol is best for smaller IP based network?

Answer:

a) RIP (Routing Information Protocol)

b) It is based on Distance Vector Routing

c) Based on the hop count, the best route is determined

144: What are the limitations of RIP v1?

Answer:

The limitations are:

a) It is reachable within 15 hops only

b) Since it is a Classful routing protocol, subnetting of a network is not possible

c) It considers only the hop count not the bandwidth

145: What are the features of RIPv2?

Answer:

Its features are:

a) Supports classless addressing and variable length subnet masking

b) Provides authentication. A router receives the packet only after its authentication is verified

c) Next intended router's IP is included in the RIP entry

d) RIP entry contains the route tag that stores the information regarding the route

146: What are the limitations of RIPv2?

Answer:

Its limitations are:

a) Hop count. It is the main drawback in both version 1 and 2

b) Using RIPv2 also, only 15 hops are reachable

OSPF Routing Protocol

147: Which protocol is used as Interior Gateway Protocol?

Answer:

a) OSPF (Open Shortest Path First)

b) It is Link-state routing protocol. Sends the LAS (link state advertisements) to all the routers in the same area

c) LAS contains information regarding metrics used, attached interfaces, etc

148: What are the disadvantages of OSPF?

Answer:

The disadvantages of OSPF are:

a) Since it uses SPF algorithm, routing information are stored in multiple copies. So, more memory is needed

b) Implementation is complex when compared to RIP

149: Give an example of OSPF.

Answer:

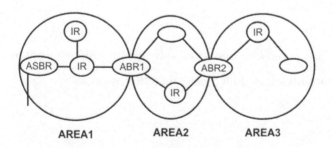

IR - Internal Router | **ABR** - Area Border Router

ASBR - Autonomous System Boundary Router

150: Describe Type 1 and Type 2 of link state advertisement.

Answer:

Type 1: The generated advertisements are linked together by the router for each area. This LSA are broadcasted to single area only

Type 2: Set routers attached to a particular network are determined from the network link advertisement generated by designated routers. Broadcasted to the area that contains this network

151: Describe about Type 3 and Type 4 of link state advertisement.

Answer:

   a) Summary Link Advertisement

   b) Inter area routes are described and generated by ABR

   c) It is for summarization and routes to the network

   d) Routes to ASBR are described by Type 4

152: Which type of LSA is used to provide links that are external to the autonomous system?

Answer:

   a) Type 5

   b) Generated by Autonomous System Boundary Router

   c) Broadcasted to all areas other stubby areas

Chapter 13

Ethernet Virtual LANs (VLAN)

153: Which of the below is equivalent to a VLAN?

a) Collision domain

b) Routing domain

c) Broadcast domain

d) Switches domain

Answer:

c) Broadcast domain

154: List at least two benefits of creating VLANs.

Answer:

The benefits of creating VLANs are:

a) VLANs segment devices into smaller LANs (broadcast
domains) to reduce overhead caused by broadcast to each

host in the VLAN

b) Network administrators can enforce better security by keeping hosts that work with sensitive data on a separate VLAN

c) VLANs organize the network by grouping users by function rather than by location

155: What is a trunk?

Answer:

A trunk is a type of switch port that allows switches to pass frames from multiple VLANs over a single physical connection. Cisco switches support two type of trunking protocols, ISL (which is Cisco proprietary) and 802.1Q.

156: Which of the below are valid VTP modes?

a) **Server**

b) **Client**

c) **Transport**

d) **Transparent**

Answer:

a) Server, b) Client, d) Transparent

157: Which command below can you use to configure VLAN "20" in a switch?

a) **vlan 20**

b) **configure vlan 20**

c) **new vlan 20**

d) create vlan 20

Answer:

a) vlan 20

158: Which command do you use to assign a switch port in VLAN "5"?

    a) assign vlan 5

    b) join vlan 5

    c) switchport access vlan 5

    d) Switchport assign vlan 5

Answer:

c) switchport access vlan 5

159: Which command do you use to set the switch port mode to trunk?

    a) switchport trunk

    b) switchport mode trunk

    c) interface trunk

    d) port mode trunk

Answer:

b) switchport mode trunk

This page is intentionally left blank

Chapter **14**

Spanning-Tree Protocol

160: How spanning tree Root Bridge is elected in layer 2 networks?

Answer:

The Root Bridge is the switch with the lowest bridge ID on the network. The bridge ID consists of two parts: switch priority and MAC address. The switches' priority is first checked to determine the lowest priority switch to be the root bridge. If there is a tie, the switches' MAC addresses are checked to determine the lowest MAC switch to be the root bridge.

161: Which of the below are valid IEEE 802.1d Spanning-Tree protocol port states?

  a) Blocking
  b) Listening

c) Adjusting

d) Forwarding

Answer:

a) Blocking, b) Listening, d) Forwarding

162: What is the benefit of Etherchannel?

Answer:

Etherchannel is useful feature in layer 2 switched networks. Etherchannel combines multiple parallel links of equal speed and type between the same pair of switches. Bundling multiple links increases bandwidth between the switches and achieves redundancy in case of one link failure.

163: What is the function of spanning-tree Portfast?

Answer:

Portfast is a feature in Spanning Tree Protocol that allows a switch to immediately place a port in Forwarding State when the port becomes physically active.

164: Which STP port role do ports of the root bridge use?

a) Root

b) Designated

c) Backup

d) Disabled

Answer:

b) Designated

165: You want to change spanning-tree Bridge ID value on a Cisco switch, which command below will you use to do that?

a) Bridge id "id"

b) Switch id "id"

c) spanning-tree vlan "num" priority "id"

d) Spanning-tree vlan "num" bridge "id"

Answer:

c) spanning-tree vlan "num" priority "id"

This page is intentionally left blank

Chapter **15**

Troubleshooting LAN Switching

166: You want to disable CDP on a specific switch. Which command do you use?

  a) No cdp run
  b) Disable cdp
  c) Remove cdp
  d) No cdp enable

Answer:

d) No cdp enable

167: A switch port is in the "down down" status. Which of the below are possible problems in that interface?

a) Bad cable

b) Layer2 protocol problem

c) The interface is disabled

d) Wrong cable pinouts

Answer:

a) Bad cable, d) Wrong cable pinouts

168: You want to view the MAC addresses learned by the switch. Which command do you use?

a) Show mac address-table

b) Show learned mac

c) Show mac table

d) Show layer2 address

Answer:

a) Show mac address-table

169: What is DHCP?

Answer:

DHCP or Dynamic Host Configuration Protocol assigns the dynamic IP to a workstation in a network. The server finds out the network address, subnet mask and gateway using DHCP and assigns a dynamic IP address based on all these and the range of allowed IP addresses in a given network. DHCP renders a reliable dynamic IP address and also helps to maintain a trouble-free TCP/IP network. The centralized assignment of IP address makes it more or less flawless and efficient.

170: Describe the function of ICMP.

Answer:

Internet Control Message Protocol (ICMP) is a vital tool in network troubleshooting. It is a protocol used to test network connectivity between network devices by sending control messages to a destination and then analyze the reply. The "ping" command uses ICMP protocol and is used to test connectivity in the network.

171: Which of the below trunking protocols support native VLAN?

a) 802.1q

b) 802.11a

c) ISL

d) 802.1n

Answer:

a) 802.1q

172: Which trunking protocol below encapsulates the Ethernet frame into a new layer 2 header and trailer?

a) 802.3

b) 802.1q

c) 802.11q

d) ISL

Answer:

d) ISL

This page is intentionally left blank

Chapter **16**

Static Routing

173: What does the character "S" means in the routing table?

Answer:

A route starting with the "S" character is a static route configured with the command "ip route".

174: Which route is preferred by a router, a Static route or OSPF learned route? Why?

Answer:

The router will use administrative distance to select one route. The lower the administrative distance, better the route. Static routes have administrative distance of "1" while OSPF routes have administrative distance of "110". So, the static route will be selected.

175: What is the default Maximum Transmission Unit (MTU) of Ethernet interface?

a) 1000 bytes

b) 150 bytes

c) 10000 bytes

d) 1500 bytes

Answer:

d) 1500 bytes

Chapter **17**

VLSM and Route Summarization

176: What is VLSM and what does it mean in the networking terminology?

Answer:

Variable Length Subnet Mask (VLSM) is a term used to describe the feature of using variable mask length in a single Class A, B, or C network instead of using the default mask of these classes. As the subnet mask is not fixed length, VLSM mandates sending the subnet mask in the routing update of routing protocols.

177: Which routing protocols below support VLSM?

  a) RIPv1
  b) OSPF

c) IGRP

d) RIPv2

Answer:

b) OSPF, d) RIPv2

178: Which subnet mask would you use over point-to-point WAN links and why?

Answer:

Point-to-point links connect only two end devices to each other requiring only two IP addresses. To preserve network addresses, the /30 mask is recommended to be used over point-to-point links to provide these two IP addresses.

179: What is route summarization and what are the benefits of it?

Answer:

Route summarization is a method to consolidate selected multiple routes into a single route advertisement. This improves routing performance as the router takes less time searching for a matching route in the routing table and saves router memory by storing less routing information.

180: What is the broadcast address of the subnet 183.15.32.0/20?

   a) **183.15.32.255**

   b) **183.15.32.254**

   c) **183.15.31.255**

   d) **183.15.74.255**

Answer:

d) 183.15.74.255

181: Which routing protocols below support Manual route summarization?

   a) **OSPF**

   b) **EIGRP**

   c) **RIPv1**

   d) **RIPv2**

Answer:

a) OSPF, b) EIGRP, d) RIPv2

This page is intentionally left blank

Chapter **18**

Control Network Traffic with Access Control Lists (ACLs)

182: What is the function of IP Access Control List (ACL)?

Answer:

IP Access Control List (ACL) is used by the router to allow or discard packets as they enter or leave an interface based on criteria defined by the network engineer. ACLs are either Standard or Extended. Standard ACL can match only on source IP address while Extended ACL can match on several parameters including source/destination IP address and source/destination port number.

183: Where is the recommended ACL application point in the network for ACLs?

Answer:

Standard ACLs should be placed as close as possible to the packet's destination because they match on the traffic's source only. Extended ACLs should be placed as close as possible to the packet's source because they can match on the traffic's source and destination hence can preserve network bandwidth.

184: What is the benefit of Extended ACL over Standard ACL?

Answer:

Extended ACL can examine multiple parts of the packet headers such as source IP, destination IP, source port and destination port while Standard ACL can examine only source IP address. Hence Extended ACLs give network administrator more control over network traffic passing through routers.

185: Which of the below can be used as matching criteria in Extended ACL?

a) Source IP address

b) Source port

c) Destination IP address

d) All of the above

Answer:

d) All of the above

Chapter **19**

OSPF Concepts

186: Which OSPF multicast address do routers send hello packet to?

    a)   224.0.0.10

    b)   224.0.0.11

    c)   224.1.1.9

    d)   224.0.0.5

Answer

d) 224.0.0.5

187: To form neighbor relationship in OSPF, two routers must agree on some parameters. Which of the below must match before two routers become neighbors?

    a)   Router ID

b) Subnet mask used on the subnet

c) Hello interval

d) Number of interfaces

Answer:

b) Subnet mask used on the subnet, c) Hello interval

188: What is OSPF "Hello Interval"?

Answer:

OSPF "Hello Interval" is the time between two successive Hello messages sent to the neighbor as a keep-alive for maintaining neighbor relationship.

189: How do you define OSPF ABR router?

Answer:

OSPF Area Border Router (ABR) is a router with interfaces connected to the backbone area and to at least one other area.

190: What is OSPF Inter-area route?

Answer:

Inter-area route is a route to a subnet in another area of which the router is not a part.

191: You want to statically configure OSPF router ID. Which command below will you use?

a) set router id "id"

b) router-id "id"

c) static id "id"

d) permanent id "id"

Answer:

b) router-id "id"

192: Which of the below is used to calculate OSPF route cost?

a) Bandwidth

b) Delay

c) MTU

d) All of the above

Answer:

a) Bandwidth

193: OSPF authentication is an important feature to secure OSPF domain. What authentication types are supported by OSPF?

a) Null authentication

b) Simple text password

c) MD5

d) All of the above

Answer:

d) All of the above

194: By default, how many OSPF equal-cost routes can be inserted in the routing table for load balancing?

a) 4

b) 6

c) 8

d) 16

Answer:

a) 4

This page is intentionally left blank

Chapter 20

EIGRP Concepts

195: In order for EIGRP neighbor relationship to form, which of the below must be validated?

a) Same AS number

b) Source IP address in Hello must be in the same subnet

c) Same Router ID

d) MTU

Answer:

a) Same AS number, b) Source IP address in Hello must be in the same subnet

196: List at least three characteristics of PPP.

Answer:

The characteristics of PPP are:

a) Multilink support for traffic load balance

b) Support for both synchronous and asynchronous links

c) Looped link detection through the magic number

d) Definition of a header and trailer that allows delivery of a data frame over the link

e) It contains a protocol type field in the header, allowing multiple Layer 3 protocols to pass over the same link

f) Support of CHAP and PAP authentication

197: Which of the below is used by default in EIGRP metric calculation?

a) **MTU**

b) **Bandwidth**

c) **Cost**

d) **Delay**

Answer:

b) Bandwidth, d) Delay

198: What is EIGRP feasible distance?

Answer:

Feasible distance is the composite metric that is used by EIGRP to select the best path(s). When there are multiple paths to the same destination received by an EIGRP router, it compares the Feasible Distance of each path, and the lowest one becomes the Successor route, which is put into the routing table.

199: What is the feasible successor route in EIGRP?

Answer:

It is alternative, immediately usable route that is used if the best route (successor route) failed. A feasible successor route has higher distance than the successor route.

200: Which of the below algorithms is used by EIGRP to recover a failed route with no feasible successor?

　a) SPF

　b) DUAL

　c) Dijekstra

　d) First Match

Answer:

b) DUAL

201: How do you define a new EIGRP process on a router with AS 1?

　a) eigrp as 1

　b) eigrp domain 1

　c) Ip eigrp 1

　d) router eigrp 1

Answer:

d) router eigrp 1

202: Which authentication types below are supported by EIGRP?

　a) Null authentication

　b) Simple text password

c) **MD5**

d) **All of the above**

Answer:

c) MD5

203: What types of load balancing does EIGRP support?

Answer:

EIGRP supports equal-cost routes load balance over 4 routes by default. EIGRP also supports unequal-cost load balancing using the variance command which defines the metric multiplier. The lowest route metric along with the variance are used to define the highest route metric. Any route that has a metric lower than this value will be used in load balancing.

Chapter 21

Point-to-Point WAN Links and Protocols

204: At which OSI reference model layer does PPP operate?

a) Layer 1

b) Layer 2

c) Layer 3

d) Layer 4

Answer:

b) Layer 2

205: Which of the below are functions of PPP LCP?

a) Looped link detection

b) Multilink support

c) **Packet retransmission**

d) **Header definition**

Answer:

a) Looped link detection, b) Multilink support

206: Which of the below are PPP authentication types?

a) **CHAP**

b) **MD5**

c) **PAP**

d) **AES**

Answer:

a) CHAP, c) PAP

207: What is the function of PPP multilink?

Answer:

PPP multilink is a feature in PPP protocol which allows the network administrator to load balance traffic over multiple parallel links to increase bandwidth and achieve redundancy instead of depending on the higher layer protocols.

208: What is the function of the "Protocol" field in PPP?

Answer:

The "Protocol" field in PPP identifies the type of packet inside the Frame. This field allows packets from the many different Layer 3 protocols to pass over a single link.

Chapter **22**

Frame-Relay Configuration and Troubleshooting

209: What is Frame-relay?

Answer:

Frame relay protocol works on the datalink and physical layers of a network. It creates and maintains permanent virtual circuits or PVC that ensures seamless connection without requiring a dedicated leased line. It puts data in frames that come in varied sized depending upon the requirement. Error-correction is done at the sending or receiving ends only which makes the transmission much faster. Special equipment such as DTE (Data Terminal Equipment) and DCE (Data Circuit-terminating Equipment) are required to set up Frame-relay.

210: What is Frame Relay LMI protocol?

Answer:

Local Management Interface (LMI) is a protocol that defines the exchange of regular keep-alive messages between the DTE (customer router) and Frame Relay switch.

211: What is the function of DLCI in Frame-relay?

Answer:

Data-link connection identifier (DLCI) is a vital component in frame-relay. It is the layer 2 address used in Frame Relay headers to identify the Permanent Virtual Circuit (PVC) and it is similar to IP address in the network layer.

212: How does frame-relay deal with broadcast?

Answer:

Frame-relay doesn't support broadcast in the same way as LAN broadcast. In Frame Relay, the broadcast is simulated by sending copies of a broadcast frame over all PVCs that are connected to the router and intended to receive it.

213: What is the FECN bit in Frame Relay and what does it mean to set it to 1?

Answer:

Forward Explicit Congestion Notification (FECN) bit is a special bit in Frame Relay header which is used in congestion management. If set, that indicates to the receiver that congestion exists in the path from the sender to it.

214: What is DE bit of frame-relay header and when it is set?

Answer:

Discard Eligibility (DE) bit is a bit in frame-relay frame header. It is used to mark frames that are less important.

This bit is used by provider's switches in case of congestion to discard frames that have this bit set. This bit is set by the customer router before sending it to the provider's switch.

215: Which of the below are valid frame-relay LMI types?

a) Cisco

b) ARIN

c) ANSI

d) ANU

Answer:

a) Cisco, c) ANSI

216: Which of the below are valid frame-relay encapsulation types?

a) ANSI

b) Cisco

c) LMI

d) IETF

Answer:

b) Cisco, d) IETF

217: What command do you use to select the interface encapsulation as frame-relay?

  a) encapsulation frame-relay

  b) frame-relay encapsulation

  c) type frame-relay

  d) frame-relay mode

Answer:

a) encapsulation frame-relay

218: Which command below will you use to set an address for frame-relay virtual circuit?

  a) circuit address "address"

  b) frame-relay address "address"

  c) frame-relay interface-dlci "address"

  d) IP address "address"

Answer:

c) frame-relay interface-dlci "address"

219: What is the function of Inverse ARP?

Answer:

The function of inverse ARP is as follows:

  a) The mapping will be created between the layer2 (DLCI) and layer3 (IP) address

  b) The result produced is same as that of Internet Protocol ARP on LAN

Chapter **23**

Virtual Private Networks (VPN)

220: Which of the below are valid VPN types?

   a) Intranet VPN

   b) Extranet VPN

   c) Access VPN

   d) HUB VPN

Answer:

a) Intranet VPN, b) Extranet VPN, c) Access VPN

221: Virtual Private Networks (VPN) provide data integrity. What is data integrity?

Answer:

Data integrity is verifying that the packet was not changed as the packet transited the Internet. Using encryption, the attacker can't decrypt the packet and hence can't change its content.

222: Which of the below are benefits of Virtual Private Networks (VPN)?

  a) Authentication
  b) Compression
  c) Caching
  d) Privacy

Answer:

a) Authentication, d) Privacy

223: Which of the below are valid VPN encryption algorithms?

  a) CHAP
  b) 3DES
  c) AES
  d) ND5

Answer:

b) 3DES, c) AES

224: How do VPNs achieve data privacy?

Answer:

Data privacy is preventing any one in the middle of internet from reading the packet's content. Using encryption, an attacker can't decrypt the packet and hence can't read its content.

Chapter **24**

Network Address Translation (NAT)

225: What are the benefits of using Network Address Translation (NAT)?

Answer:

The benefits of using Network Address Translation are:

a) As private IP addresses can't be used over internet, NAT allows hosts assigned private IP addresses to access internet by translating their private IP addresses to public IP addresses

b) Lessens the need for additional globally routable address space for internal hosts

c) Increases network security by hiding company's internal IP addresses

226: Which of the below are private IP address?

   a) **192.168.23.22**

   b) **172.14.23.9**

   c) **10.110.23.22**

   d) **41.343.22.34**

Answer:

a) 192.168.23.22, c) 10.110.23.22

227: In NAT terminology, what does the term Inside Global mean?

Answer:

Inside Global is the IP address of inside host (inside local IP addresses) as viewed by the outside world. An example of it is the public IP address used to NAT inside user IP address. This public IP is "Inside Global" address as viewed by internet users.

228: What is PAT?

Answer:

Port Address Translation (PAT) is a type of NAT in which a single IP address is used to NAT several clients' IP addresses with different port numbers per client session.

229: Which command do you use to clear the dynamic entries in the router's NAT table?

   a) **clear nat table dynamic**

   b) **clear dynamic nat**

   c) **clear ip nat translations ***

   d) **remove dynamic nat**

Answer:

c) clear ip nat translations *

Chapter **25**

IP Version 6 (IPv6)

230: What are the advantages of using IPv6?

Answer:

The advantages of using IPv6 are:

a) It allows for a very large addressing space to support more network devices

b) It removes the need for NAT/PAT which avoids complexity of configuring NAT/PAT

c) It improves network security as some security features are built in IPv6

231: What is IPv6 Anycast IP address?

Answer:

An IPv6 Anycast IP address is a design choice by which servers that support the same function can use the same unicast IP address. An Anycast address is a single address assigned to multiple nodes. A packet sent to an Anycast address is then delivered to the first available node.

232: Select the shortest valid abbreviation for the IPv6 address FE90:0000:0000:0650:0000:0000:0000:0564.

a) FE90::0650::564
b) FE90:0000:0000:0650::0564
c) FE90:0000:0000:650::564
d) FE9:0000:0000:65::564

Answer:

c) FE90:0000:0000:650::564

233: Which of the below are IPv6 routing protocols?

a) RIPv6
b) RIPng
c) OSPFv3
d) OSPFv6

Answer:

b) RIPng, c) OSPFv3

234: What is IPv6 EUI-64 address format?

Answer:

The IPv6 device reconfigures the 48-bit MAC address into a 64-bit Extended Unique Identifier (EUI) or the Interface ID which will be unique. The conversion is made possible by inserting 'FFFE' in the middle of the MAC address. The 7th bit, which is a Universal/Local identifier, is then inverted. If the 7th bit is 0, it becomes 1 and vice versa.

Chapter **26**

Subnet Masking

235: How will you compute network and host part of the given IP address say 192.194.211.078?

Answer:

We can compute network and host part of the given IP address using 'And' on the given IP address and subnet mask.

Since the given IP comes under the range of 192 to 223, it belongs to class C.

IP: (AND) 1100 0000 1000 0010 1001 0011 0100 1110

Default subnet mask 1111 1111 1111 1111 1111 1111 0000 0000

1100 0000 1000 0010 1001 0011 0000 0000

Network Part: 192.194.211.000

Host Part: 078

236: What does it mean when network address is all 0's or 1's?

Answer:

a) All 1's: Of the form: N/w.N/w.H.H

    1111.1111.1100.0010

    It means it belongs to all networks

b) All 0's: of the form: N/w.N/w.H.H

    0000.0000.1100.0010

    Belongs to that particular network/segment

237: What is called classless Inter Domain Routing?

Answer:

To get the number of networks in the IP, default subnet mask is used. The subnet mask does not have host part for Classful masking,

However, subnet mask contains the host part in classless subnet masking. This is called Classless Inter Domain Routing (CIDR).

This increases the number of networks for the given network address.

238: Calculate the number of host and subnets for the given IP address (158.220.78.24) with subnet mask of 7 bits.

Answer:

a) The given IP comes under 'class B' addressing of the form N/w.N/w.H.H

b) The default subnet masking is 16 bits

c) Given subnets-6 bits. Hence (16 + 7 = 23 bits)

d) For host, 32 − 23 = 9 bits, i.e. $2^9 − 2 = 510$) host

e) For subnets, ($2^7 − 2 = 126$) subnets

239: What is the use of CIDR?

Answer:

An IP address is assigned to each individual. It is not possible to allocate IP for each individual with the use of Classful addressing. Hence CIDR is used. It provides a pool of IP's to Internet service providers (ISP). Then the internet service provider allocates the IP to their customer from the given pool. This provides the efficient utilization of internet

This page is intentionally left blank

Chapter **27**

Networks and Protocols

240: What is converged network?

Answer:

In a converged network, different types of communicating devices such as telephones, computer, television uses a common network to communicate their voice, data, video following the same rules. Example of this network is the internet.

241: Explain session layer with a real time example.

Answer:

Session layer is the one which is responsible for making up and ending a connection when a session is created. For example, in messenger like Google Talk a session is created every time when we open a new window for the chat. In this case, the session layer creates the connection to the Google server and removes the connection when not needed.

242: What is a port?

Answer:

a) A file pointer is a port

b) All the request received at the port is stored in a buffer, so the port is logical

c) Buffer is a file

d) The server checks the buffer file for the request

243: For the following services provide their corresponding protocols:

a) **WWW**

b) **Instant Message**

c) **E-mail**

d) **IP telephony**

Answer:

a) WWW-HTTP (Hypertext Transport Protocol)

b) E-mail –SMTP, POP

c) Instant message- XMPP, OSCAR

d) IP telephony- SIP

244: What is the use of "show ipx servers" command?

Answer:

It is used to find the names of Novell servers on a network.

245: Describe about communication protocol.

Answer:

a) Communication protocol tells the set of rules to communicate between the hardware devices

b) Communication protocol can be of both as software and hardware

246: Is it wise to set a single protocol to handle all data communication? If not, what action is to be taken to solve this problem?

Answer:

No, instead the protocol software has been arranged in different layers so that each layer handles a particular set of problems.

247: What is Fault tolerance?

Answer:

Fault Tolerance is a property by which the network continues to function even though some of its components fail. Redundancy is a key factor of Fault tolerance. If a server fails, redundant server performs its function until the server is repaired.

248: Describe the two authentication protocols in PPP.

Answer:

a) PAP uses two-way handshake process. It sends username and password in clear text. If a match is found with the stored username and password it accepts else rejects. Normally used on FTP sites

b) CHAP uses three handshake process. It employs encryption

and is the most secure way

249: What is P2P network and their application?

Answer:

In Peer-to-Peer network, two or more computers connected through a network can share their information such as printers, files. They don't require a separate dedicated server. Each computer is called as a peer. Peer can act as a server or a client. Applications of P2P network include P2P hybrid system, client-server networks, internet.

250: What are the types of record stored in DNS?

Answer:

a) A

b) NS

c) CNAME

d) MX

251: In case of sharing large messages which process is employed?

Answer:

The process is called Segmentation. Segmentation splits the message into smaller parts that travel through different routes to reach the destination. It also has the advantage of multiplexing and increasing the efficiency of the network communication.

252: How is Corruption of data is prevented?

Answer:

Corruption of data is prevented through Encapsulation. Encapsulation adds control information at each layer. Data at each level is called as Protocol Data Unit (PDU). PDU is different at each layer. Layer 1 PDU is a bit while layer 2 PDU is a frame.

253: Point the difference between VTY and AYT.

Answer:

Connection using Telnet is VTY (Virtual Terminal) session. Are You There (AYT) is Telnet protocol command. Usually occurs as an icon indicating the Telnet connection is active.

254: What is the use of netsat?

Answer:

Command showing the local address, destination address, port number, protocol in use and the state of a connection. It is normally used to verify the TCP connections. It can be used to check open connections. Connections which cannot be explained can indicate someone is connected to the host indicating security threat.

255: What is the purpose of setting the TTL value?

Answer:

An 8-bit field found in the IP header. Its value is set by the sender device. The purpose of setting its value is to prevent the circulation of the undeliverable packet in the network. Each time it visits a router, its value is decreased by one. So, the time packet reaches the destination device, TTL value will be zero.

256: What is SMB?

Answer:

SMB is Server Message Block Protocol; it helps to access files at a remote server including printers, mailslots, and named pipes. Microsoft has provided open source version of SMB called CIFS (Common Internet File System), which is more flexible than FTP.

257: Why IPV4 network is also referred as broadcast domain?

Answer:

Limited broadcast is only for hosts on the local network. Routers do not forward this broadcast. On the local network, packets with limited broadcast will only exist.

258: What are the early versions of the Ethernet?

Answer:

a)   Thicknet (10BASE5) – uses thick co-axial cables for about 500 meters

b)   Thinnet (10BASE2) – uses thin co-axial cable for about 185 meters

259: What is the advantage of the switch over a hub in Ethernet?

Answer:

The advantages of a switch over a hub in Ethernet are:

a)   Increases the throughput

b)   Posses higher bandwidth

c) Collision-free

d) Increased performance

260: What is goodput?

Answer:

Goodput is the transfer rate of actual usable bits. It is a throughput minus traffic overhead for establishing sessions, acknowledgments, and encapsulation. It doesn't consider retransmissions. Factors that cause lower goodput than throughput is protocol overhead, corrupt packets, transport layer flow control and congestion avoidance.

This page is intentionally left blank

Chapter **28**

Cisco IOS

261: What is 'user EXEC level'?

Answer:

a) It is a level that will be provided for the users initially

b) Provides access only to small number of basic monitoring commands

c) Symbol used to denote this command is '>'

262: When a user can get into the privileged EXEC level?

Answer:

a) 'User EXEC level' is the basic level. When the user enters this level, they will be asked for password

b) By providing the correct password, they can enter into privileged EXEC level

c) This level provides access to all the router commands

263: Describe about 'Global' and 'Interface' configuration mode.

Answer:

Global configuration mode:

a) Systems' configuration can be changed by the users when they are in the 'global configuration mode'

b) Represented by '(config)#'

Interface configuration mode:

a) Configuration of the interface can be changed by the user when they are in the 'Interface Configuration Mode'

b) Represented by '(config-in)#'

HR Interview Questions

Review these typical interview questions and think about how you would answer them. Read the answers listed; you will find best possible answers along with strategies and suggestions.

1: Where do you find ideas?

Answer:

Ideas can come from all places, and an interviewer wants to see that your ideas are just as varied. Mention multiple places that you gain ideas from, or settings in which you find yourself brainstorming. Additionally, elaborate on how you record ideas or expand upon them later.

2: How do you achieve creativity in the workplace?

Answer:

It's important to show the interviewer that you're capable of being resourceful and innovative in the workplace, without stepping outside the lines of company values. Explain where ideas normally stem from for you (examples may include an exercise such as list-making or a mind map), and connect this to a particular task in your job that it would be helpful to be creative in.

3: How do you push others to create ideas?

Answer:

If you're in a supervisory position, this may be requiring employees to submit a particular number of ideas, or to complete regular idea-generating exercises, in order to work their creative muscles. However, you can also push others around you to create ideas simply by creating more of your own. Additionally, discuss with the interviewer the importance of questioning people as a way to inspire ideas and change.

4: Describe your creativity.

Answer:

Try to keep this answer within the professional realm, but if you have an impressive background in something creative outside of your employment history, don't be afraid to include it in your answer also. The best answers about creativity will relate problem-solving skills, goal-setting, and finding innovative ways to tackle a project or make a sale in the workplace. However, passions outside of the office are great, too (so long as they don't cut into your work time or mental space).

5: How would you handle a negative coworker?

Answer:

Everyone has to deal with negative coworkers – and the single best way to do so is to remain positive. You may try to build a relationship with the coworker or relate to them in some way, but even if your efforts are met with a cold shoulder, you must retain your positive attitude. Above all, stress that you would never allow a coworker's negativity to impact your own work or productivity.

6: What would you do if you witnessed a coworker surfing the web, reading a book, etc, wasting company time?

Answer:

The interviewer will want to see that you realize how detrimental it is for employees to waste company time, and that it is not something you take lightly. Explain the way you would adhere to company policy, whether that includes talking to the coworker yourself, reporting the behavior straight to a supervisor, or talking to someone in HR.

7: How do you handle competition among yourself and other employees?

Answer:

Healthy competition can be a great thing, and it is best to stay focused on the positive aspects of this here. Don't bring up conflict among yourself and other coworkers, and instead focus on the motivation to keep up with the great work of others, and the ways in which coworkers may be a great support network in helping to push you to new successes.

8: When is it okay to socialize with coworkers?

Answer:

This question has two extreme answers (all the time, or never), and your interviewer, in most cases, will want to see that you fall somewhere in the middle. It's important to establish solid relationships with your coworkers, but never at the expense of getting work done. Ideally, relationship-building can happen with exercises of teamwork and special projects, as well as in the break room.

9: Tell me about a time when a major change was made at your last job, and how you handled it.

Answer:

Provide a set-up for the situation including the old system, what the change was, how it was implemented, and the results of the change, and include how you felt about each step of the way. Be sure that your initial thoughts on the old system are neutral, and that your excitement level grows with each step of the new change, as an interviewer will be pleased to see your adaptability.

10: When delegating tasks, how do you choose which tasks go to which team members?

Answer:

The interviewer is looking to gain insight into your thought process with this question, so be sure to offer thorough reasoning behind your choice. Explain that you delegate tasks based on each individual's personal strengths, or that you look at how many other projects each person is working on at the time, in order to create the best fit possible.

11: Tell me about a time when you had to stand up for something you believed strongly about to coworkers or a supervisor.

Answer:

While it may be difficult to explain a situation of conflict to an interviewer, this is a great opportunity to display your passions and convictions, and your dedication to your beliefs. Explain not just the situation to the interviewer, but also elaborate on why it was so important to you to stand up for the issue, and how your coworker or supervisor responded to you afterward – were they more respectful? Unreceptive? Open-minded? Apologetic?

12: Tell me about a time when you helped someone finish their work, even though it wasn't "your job."

Answer:

Though you may be frustrated when required to pick up someone else's slack, it's important that you remain positive about lending a hand. The interviewer will be looking to see if you're a team player, and by helping someone else finish a task that he or she couldn't manage alone, you show both your willingness to help the team succeed, and your own competence.

13: What are the challenges of working on a team? How do you handle this?

Answer:

There are many obvious challenges to working on a team, such as handling different perspectives, navigating individual schedules, or accommodating difficult workers. It's best to focus on one challenge, such as individual team members missing deadlines or failing to keep commitments, and then offer a solution that clearly addresses the problem. For example, you could organize weekly status meetings for your team to discuss progress or assign shorter deadlines in order to keep the long-term deadline on schedule.

14: Do you value diversity in the workplace?

Answer:

Diversity is important in the workplace in order to foster an environment that is accepting, equalizing, and full of different perspectives and backgrounds. Be sure to show your awareness of these issues and stress the importance of learning from others' experiences.

15: How would you handle a situation in which a coworker was not accepting of someone else's diversity?

Answer:

Explain that it is important to adhere to company policies regarding diversity, and that you would talk to the relevant supervisors or management team. When it is appropriate, it could also be best to talk to the coworker in question about the benefits of alternate perspectives – if you can handle the situation yourself, its best not to bring resolvable issues to management.

16: Are you rewarded more from working on a team, or accomplishing a task on your own?

Answer:

It's best to show a balance between these two aspects – your employer wants to see that you're comfortable working on your own, and that you can complete tasks efficiently and well without assistance. However, it's also important for your employer to see that you can be a team player, and that you understand the value that multiple perspectives and efforts can bring to a project.

17: Tell me about a time when you didn't meet a deadline.

Answer:

Ideally, this hasn't happened – but if it has, make sure you use a minor example to illustrate the situation, emphasize how long ago it happened, and be sure that you did as much as you could to ensure that the deadline was met. Additionally, be sure to include what you learned about managing time better or prioritizing tasks in order to meet all future deadlines.

18: How do you eliminate distractions while working?

Answer:

With the increase of technology and the ease of communication, new distractions arise every day. Your interviewer will want to see that you are still able to focus on work, and that your productivity has not been affected, by an example showing a routine you employ in order to stay on task.

19: Tell me about a time when you worked in a position with a weekly or monthly quota to meet. How often were you successful?

Answer:

Your numbers will speak for themselves, and you must answer this question honestly. If you were regularly met your quotas, be sure to highlight this in a confident manner and don't be shy in pointing out your strengths in this area. If your statistics are less than stellar, try to point out trends in which they increased toward the end of your employment, and show reflection as to ways you can improve in the future.

20: Tell me about a time when you met a tough deadline, and how you were able to complete it.

Answer:

Explain how you were able to prioritize tasks, or to delegate portions of assignments to other team members, in order to deal with a tough deadline. It may be beneficial to specify why the deadline was tough – make sure it's clear that it was not a result of procrastination on your part. Finally, explain how you were able to successfully meet the deadline, and what it took to get there in the end.

21: How do you stay organized when you have multiple projects on your plate?

Answer:

The interviewer will be looking to see that you can manage your time and work well – and being able to handle multiple projects at once, and still giving each the attention it deserves, is a great mark of a worker's competence and efficiency. Go through a typical process of goal-setting and prioritizing, and explain the steps of these to the interviewer, so he or she can see how well you manage time.

22: How much time during your work day do you spend on "auto-pilot?"

Answer:

While you may wonder if the employer is looking to see how efficient you are with this question (for example, so good at your job that you don't have to think about it), but in almost every case, the employer wants to see that you're constantly thinking, analyzing, and processing what's going on in the workplace. Even if things are running smoothly, there's usually an opportunity somewhere to make things more efficient or to increase sales or productivity. Stress your dedication to ongoing development and convey that being on "auto-pilot" is not conducive to that type of success.

23: How do you handle deadlines?

Answer:

The most important part of handling tough deadlines is to prioritize tasks and set goals for completion, as well as to delegate or eliminate unnecessary work. Lead the interviewer through a general scenario and display your competency through your ability to organize and set priorities, and most importantly, remain calm.

24: Tell me about your personal problem-solving process.

Answer:

Your personal problem-solving process should include outlining the problem, coming up with possible ways to fix the problem, and setting a clear action plan that leads to resolution. Keep your answer brief and organized, and explain the steps in a concise, calm manner that shows you are level-headed even under stress.

25: What sort of things at work can make you stressed?

Answer:

As it's best to stay away from negatives, keep this answer brief and simple. While answering that nothing at work makes you stressed will not be very believable to the interviewer, keep your answer to one generic principle such as when members of a team don't keep their commitments, and then focus on a solution you generally employ to tackle that stress, such as having weekly status meetings or intermittent deadlines along the course of a project.

26: What do you look like when you are stressed about something? How do you solve it?

Answer:

This is a trick question – your interviewer wants to hear that you don't look any different when you're stressed, and that you don't allow negative emotions to interfere with your productivity. As far as how you solve your stress, it's best if you have a simple solution mastered, such as simply taking deep breaths and counting to 10 to bring yourself back to the task at hand.

27: Can you multi-task?

Answer:

Some people can, and some people can't. The most important part of multi-tasking is to keep a clear head at all times about what needs to be done, and what priority each task falls under. Explain how you evaluate tasks to determine priority, and how you manage your time in order to ensure that all are completed efficiently.

28: How many hours per week do you work?

Answer:

Many people get tricked by this question, thinking that answering more hours is better – however, this may cause an employer to wonder why you have to work so many hours in order to get the work done that other people can do in a shorter amount of time. Give a fair estimate of hours that it should take you to complete a job and explain that you are also willing to work extra whenever needed.

29: How many times per day do you check your email?

Answer:

While an employer wants to see that you are plugged into modern technology, it is also important that the number of times you check your email per day is relatively low – perhaps two to three times per day (dependent on the specific field you're in). Checking email is often a great distraction in the workplace, and while it is important to remain connected, much correspondence can simply be handled together in the morning and afternoon.

30: What has been your biggest success?

Answer:

Your biggest success should be something that was especially meaningful to you, and that you can talk about passionately – your interviewer will be able to see this. Always have an answer prepared for this question, and be sure to explain how you achieved success, as well as what you learned from the experience.

31: What motivates you?

Answer:

It's best to focus on a key aspect of your work that you can target as a "driving force" behind your everyday work. Whether it's customer service, making a difference, or the chance to further your skills and gain experience, it's important that the interviewer can see the passion you hold for your career and the dedication you have to the position.

32: What do you do when you lose motivation?

Answer:

The best candidates will answer that they rarely lose motivation, because they already employ strategies to keep themselves inspired, and because they remain dedicated to their objectives. Additionally, you may impress the interviewer by explaining that you are motivated by achieving goals and advancing, so small successes are always a great way to regain momentum.

33: What do you like to do in your free time?

Answer:

What you do answer here is not nearly as important as what you don't answer – your interviewer does not want to hear that you like to drink, party, or revel in the nightlife. Instead, choose a few activities to focus on that are greater signs of stability and maturity, and that will not detract from your ability to show up to work and be productive, such as reading, cooking, or photography. This is also a great opportunity to show your interviewer that you are a well-rounded, interesting, and dynamic personality that they would be happy to hire.

34: What sets you apart from other workers?

Answer:

This question is a great opportunity to highlight the specific skill sets and passion you bring to the company that no one else can. If you can't outline exactly what sets you apart from other workers, how will the interviewer see it? Be prepared with a thorough outline of what you will bring to the table, in order to help the company, achieve their goals.

35: Why are you the best candidate for that position?

Answer:

Have a brief response prepared in advance for this question, as this is another very common theme in interviews (variations of the question include: "Why should I hire you, above Candidate B?" and "What can you bring to our company that Candidate B cannot?"). Make sure that your statement does not sound rehearsed and highlight your most unique qualities that show the interviewer why he or she must hire you above all the other candidates. Include specific details about your experience and special projects or recognition you've received that set you apart, and show your greatest passion, commitment, and enthusiasm for the position.

36: What does it take to be successful?

Answer:

Hard work, passion, motivation, and a dedication to learning – these are all potential answers to the ambiguous concept of success. It doesn't matter so much which of these values you choose as the primary means to success, or if you choose a combination of them. It is, however, absolutely key that whichever value you choose, you must clearly display in your attitude, experience, and goals.

37: What would be the biggest challenge in this position for you?

Answer:

Keep this answer positive and remain focused on the opportunities for growth and learning that the position can provide. Be sure that no matter what the challenge is, it's obvious that you're ready and enthusiastic to tackle it, and that you have a full awareness of what it will take to get the job done.

38: Would you describe yourself as an introvert or an extrovert?

Answer:

There are beneficial qualities to each of these, and your answer may depend on what type of work you're involved in. However, a successful leader may be an introvert or extrovert, and similarly, solid team members may also be either. The important aspect of this question is to have the level of self-awareness required to accurately describe yourself.

39: What are some positive character traits that you don't possess?

Answer:

If an interviewer asks you a tough question about your weaknesses, or lack of positive traits, it's best to keep your answer light-hearted and simple – for instance, express your great confidence in your own abilities, followed by a (rather humble) admittance that you could occasionally do to be humbler.

40: What is the greatest lesson you've ever learned?

Answer:

While this is a very broad question, the interviewer will be more interested in hearing what kind of emphasis you place on this value. Your greatest lesson may tie in with something a mentor, parent, or professor once told you, or you may have gleaned it from a book written by a leading expert in your field. Regardless of what the lesson is, it is most important that you can offer an example of how you've incorporated it into your life.

41: Have you ever been in a situation where one of your strengths became a weakness in an alternate setting?

Answer:

It's important to show an awareness of yourself by having an answer for this question, but you want to make sure that the weakness is relatively minor, and that it would still remain strength in most settings. For instance, you may be an avid reader who reads anything and everything you can find but reading billboards while driving to work may be a dangerous idea.

42: Who has been the most influential person in your life?

Answer:

Give a specific example (and name) to the person who has influenced your life greatly and offer a relevant anecdote about a meaningful exchange the two of you shared. It's great if their influence relates to your professional life, but this particular question opens up the possibility to discuss inspiration in your personal life as well. The interviewer wants to see that you're able to make strong connections with other individuals, and to work under the guiding influence of another person.

43: Do you consider yourself to be a "detailed" or "big picture" type of person?

Answer:

Both of these are great qualities, and it's best if you can incorporate each into your answer. Choose one as your primary type and relate it to experience or specific items from your resume. Then, explain how the other type fits into your work as well.

44: What is your greatest fear?

Answer:

Disclosing your greatest fear openly and without embarrassment is a great way to show your confidence to an employer. Choose a fear that you are clearly doing work to combat, such as a fear of failure that will seem impossible to the interviewer for someone such as yourself, with such clear goals and actions plans outlined. As tempting as it may be to stick with an easy answer such as spiders, stay away from these, as they don't really tell the interviewer anything about yourself that's relevant.

45: What sort of challenges do you enjoy?

Answer:

The challenges you enjoy should demonstrate some sort of initiative or growth potential on your part and should also be in line with your career objectives. Employers will evaluate consistency here, as they analyze critically how the challenges you look forward to are related to your ultimate goals.

46: Tell me about a time you were embarrassed. How did you handle it?

Answer:

No one wants to bring up times they were embarrassed in a job interview, and it's probably best to avoid an anecdote here. However, don't shy away from offering a brief synopsis, followed by a display of your ability to laugh it off. Show the interviewer that it was not an event that impacted you significantly.

47: What is your greatest weakness?

Answer:

This is another one of the most popular questions asked in job interviews, so you should be prepared with an answer already. Try to come up with a weakness that you have that can actually be a strength in an alternate setting – such as, "I'm very detail-oriented and like to ensure that things are done correctly, so I sometimes have difficulty in delegating tasks to others." However, don't try to mask obvious weaknesses – if you have little practical experience in the field, mention that you're looking forward to great opportunities to further your knowledge.

48: What are the three best adjectives to describe you in a work setting?

Answer:

While these three adjectives probably already appear somewhere on your resume, don't be afraid to use them again in order to highlight your best qualities. This is a chance for you to sell yourself to the interviewer, and to point out traits you possess that other candidates do not. Use the most specific and accurate words you can think of and elaborate shortly on how you embody each.

49: What are the three best adjectives to describe you in your personal life?

Answer:

Ideally, the three adjectives that describe you in your personal life should be similar to the adjectives that describe you in your professional life. Employers appreciate consistency, and while they may understand of you having an alternate personality outside of the office, it's best if you employ similar principles in your actions both on and off the clock.

50: What type of worker are you?

Answer:

This is an opportunity for you to highlight some of your greatest assets. Characterize some of your talents such as dedicated, self-motivated, detail-oriented, passionate, hard-working, analytical, or customer service focused. Stay away from your weaker qualities here and remain on the target of all the wonderful things that you can bring to the company.

51: Tell me about your happiest day at work.

Answer:

Your happiest day at work should include one of your greatest professional successes, and how it made you feel. Stay focused on what you accomplished and be sure to elaborate on how rewarding or satisfying the achievement was for you.

52: Tell me about your worst day at work.

Answer:

It may have been the worst day ever because of all the mistakes you made, or because you'd just had a huge argument with your best friend, but make sure to keep this answer professionally focused. Try to use an example in which something uncontrollable happened in the workplace (such as an important member of a team quit unexpectedly, which ruined your team's meeting with a client), and focus on the frustration of not being in control of the situation. Keep this answer brief and be sure to end with a reflection on what you learned from the day.

53: What are you passionate about?

Answer:

Keep this answer professionally-focused where possible, but it may also be appropriate to discuss personal issues you are passionate about as well (such as the environment or volunteering at a soup kitchen). Stick to issues that are non-controversial and allow your passion to shine through as you explain what inspires you about the topic and how you stay actively engaged in it. Additionally, if you choose a personal passion, make sure it is one that does not detract from your availability to work or to be productive.

54: What is the piece of criticism you receive most often?

Answer:

An honest, candid answer to this question can greatly impress an interviewer (when, of course, it is coupled with an explanation of what you're doing to improve), but make sure the criticism is something minimal or unrelated to your career.

55: What type of work environment do you succeed the most in?

Answer:

Be sure to research the company and the specific position before heading into the interview. Tailor your response to fit the job you'd be working in and explain why you enjoy that type of environment over others. However, it's also extremely important to be adaptable, so remain flexible to other environments as well.

56: Are you an emotional person?

Answer:

It's best to focus on your positive emotions – passion, happiness, motivations – and to stay away from other extreme emotions that may cause you to appear unbalanced. While you want to display your excitement for the job, be sure to remain level-headed and cool at all times, so that the interviewer knows you're not the type of person who lets emotions take you over and get in the way of your work.

57: Ten years ago, what were your career goals?

Answer:

In reflecting back to what your career goals were ten years ago, it's important to show the ways in which you've made progress in that time. Draw distinct links between specific objectives that you've achieved and speak candidly about how it felt to reach those goals. Remain positive, upbeat, and growth-oriented, even if you haven't yet achieved all of the goals you set out to reach.

58: Tell me about a weakness you used to have, and how you changed it.

Answer:

Choose a non-professional weakness that you used to have and outline the process you went through in order to grow past it. Explain the weakness itself, why it was problematic, the action steps you planned, how you achieved them, and the end result.

59: Tell me about your goal-setting process.

Answer:

When describing your goal-setting process, clearly outline the way that you create an outline for yourself. It may be helpful to offer an example of a particular goal you've set in the past and use this as a starting point to guide the way you created action steps, check-in points, and how the goal was eventually achieved.

60: Tell me about a time when you solved a problem by creating actionable steps to follow.

Answer:

This question will help the interviewer to see how you talented you are in outlining, problem resolution, and goal-setting. Explain thoroughly the procedure of outlining the problem, establishing steps to take, and then how you followed the steps (such as through check-in points along the way, or intermediary goals).

61: Where do you see yourself five years from now?

Answer:

Have some idea of where you would like to have advanced to in the position you're applying for, over the next several years. Make sure that your future plans line up with you still working for the company and stay positive about potential advancement. Focus on future opportunities and what you're looking forward to – but make sure your reasons for advancement are admirable, such as greater experience and the chance to learn, rather than simply being out for a higher salary.

62: When in a position, do you look for opportunities to promote?

Answer:

There's a fine balance in this question – you want to show the interviewer that you have initiative and motivation to advance in your career, but not at the expense of appearing opportunistic or selfishly-motivated. Explain that you are always open to growth opportunities, and very willing to take on new responsibilities as your career advances.

63: On a scale of 1 to 10, how successful has your life been?

Answer:

Though you may still have a long list of goals to achieve, it's important to keep this answer positively-focused. Choose a high number between 7 and 9 and explain that you feel your life has been largely successful and satisfactory as a result of several specific achievements or experiences. Don't go as high as a 10, as the interviewer may not believe your response or in your ability to reason critically.

64: What is your greatest goal in life?

Answer:

It is okay for this answer to stray a bit into your personal life, but best if you can keep it professionally-focused. While specific goals are great, if your personal goal doesn't match up exactly with one of the company's objectives, you're better off keeping your goal a little more generic and encompassing, such as "success in my career" or "leading a happy and fulfilling life." Keep your answer brief, and show a decisive nature – most importantly, make it clear that you've already thought about this question and know what you want.

65: Tell me about a time when you set a goal in your personal life and achieved it.

Answer:

The interviewer can see that you excel at setting goals in your professional life, but he or she also wants to know that you are consistent in your life and capable of setting goals outside of the office as well. Use an example such as making a goal to eat more healthily or to drink more water and discuss what steps you outlined to achieve your goal, the process of taking action, and the final results as well.

66: What is your greatest goal in your career?

Answer:

Have a very specific goal of something you want to achieve in your career in mind and be sure that it's something the position clearly puts you in line to accomplish. Offer the goal as well as your plans to get there and emphasize clear ways in which this position will be an opportunity to work toward the goal.

67: Tell me about a time when you achieved a goal.

Answer:

Start out with how you set the goal, and why you chose it. Then, take the interviewer through the process of outlining the goal, taking steps to achieve it, the outcome, and finally, how you felt after achieving it or recognition you received. The most important part of this question includes the planning and implementation of strategies, so focus most of your time on explaining these aspects. However, the preliminary decisions and end results are also important, so make sure to include them as well.

68: What areas of your work would you still like to improve in? What are your plans to do this?

Answer:

While you may not want the interviewer to focus on things you could improve on, it's important to be self-aware of your own growth opportunities. More importantly, you can impress an interviewer by having specific goals and actions outlined in order to facilitate your growth, even if your area of improvement is something as simple as increasing sales or finding new ways to create greater efficiency.

69: What is customer service?

Answer:

Customer service can be many things – and the most important consideration in this question is that you have a creative answer. Demonstrate your ability to think outside the box by offering a confident answer that goes past a basic definition, and that shows you have truly considered your own individual view of what it means to take care of your customers. The thoughtful consideration you hold for customers will speak for itself.

70: Tell me about a time when you went out of your way for a customer.

Answer:

It's important that you offer an example of a time you truly went out of your way – be careful not to confuse something that felt like a big effort on your part, with something your employer would expect you to do anyway. Offer an example of the customer's problems, what you did to solve it, and the way the customer responded after you took care of the situation.

71: How do you gain confidence from customers?

Answer:

This is a very open-ended question that allows you to show your customer service skills to the interviewer. There are many possible answers, and it is best to choose something that you've had great experience with, such as "by handling situations with transparency," "offering rewards," or "focusing on great communication." Offer specific examples of successes you've had.

72: Tell me about a time when a customer was upset or agitated – how did you handle the situation?

Answer:

Similarly, to handling a dispute with another employee, the most important part to answering this question is to first set up the scenario, offer a step-by-step guide to your particular conflict resolution style, and end by describing the way the conflict was resolved. Be sure that in answering questions about your own conflict resolution style, that you emphasize the importance of open communication and understanding from both parties, as well as a willingness to reach a compromise or other solution.

73: When can you make an exception for a customer?

Answer:

Exceptions for customers can generally be made when in accordance with company policy or when directed by a supervisor. Display an understanding of the types of situations in which an exception should be considered, such as when a customer has endured a particular hardship, had a complication with an order, or at a request.

74: What would you do in a situation where you were needed by both a customer and your boss?

Answer:

While both your customer and your boss have different needs of you and are very important to your success as a worker, it is always best to try to attend to your customer first – however, the key is explaining to your boss why you are needed urgently by the customer, and then to assure your boss that you will attend to his or her needs as soon as possible (unless it's absolutely an urgent matter).

75: What is the most important aspect of customer service?

Answer:

While many people would simply state that customer satisfaction is the most important aspect of customer service, it's important to be able to elaborate on other important techniques in customer service situations. Explain why customer service is such a key part of business and be sure to expand on the aspect that you deem to be the most important in a way that is reasoned and well-thought out.

76: Is it best to create low or high expectations for a customer?

Answer:

You may answer this question either way (after, of course, determining that the company does not have a clear opinion on the matter). However, no matter which way you answer the question, you must display a thorough thought process, and very clear reasoning for the option you chose. Offer pros and cons of each and include the ultimate point that tips the scale in favor of your chosen answer.

INDEX

CCNA Interview Questions

TCP/IP and OSI Networking Models

1:    What are the differences between TCP/IP and OCP Models?

2:    Explain Broadcast, Multicast and Unicast.

3:    What is OSI reference model "network" layer?

4:    Which of the below are Transport layer protocols?

5:    In networking terminology, what is "data encapsulation"?

6:    In which OSI reference model layer does HTTP operate?

7:    What is CSMA/CD and how does it work?

8:    What are the two kinds of transport possible and give some example?

9:    How TCP ensures a reliable as well as controlled transport?

10:   For an inherent requirement application which protocol would be better to use at the transport layer?

11:   When the client will declare that the server is unreachable if the client sends data to a server?

12:   Why the windowing concept is introduced in TCP?

13:   List the TCP/IP port for following:

14:   What are the advantages of UDP over TCP?

LAN Fundamentals

15:   Explain the Token Ring Operation.

16:   Explain FDDI.

17:   Which connector type is used in Ethernet cables?

18:   What is broadcast MAC address and what is its value?

19:   Describe "twisted" pair cables and mention why they are twisted.

20:   Describe how you can make an Ethernet cross-over cable.

21:   What typical cable type do you use to connect two switches together?

22:    What is the maximum cable length in Fast Ethernet (IEEE 802.3u) standard?

WAN Fundamentals

23:    What are these devices used for in a WAN network - Access Server, Modem and WAN Switch?

24:    What is ISDN?

25:    What are the advantages of the Layered model in networking?

26:    What is the speed of E1 line?

27:    Which of the below are OSI layer2 WAN protocols?

28:    Which of the below are types of Digital Subscriber line (DSL)?

29:    When connecting to internet, which of the below remote access technologies are considered always on?

30:    You use a DSL connection at home for internet connectivity. You use an IP address of 10.10.10.10 on your PC. The DSL is doing NAT for your IP to 41.111.23.23 to access internet. According to NAT terminology, what is the name of your IP address after being NATed to the public IP as viewed on internet?

31:    Which protocols below are layer2 protocols that can be used over WAN?

32:    Which command below do you use to configure PPP on a serial interface?

33:    When configuring Internet Access Router in small office, which features below are usually configured to allow internet access for users?

34:    Why PAT is used when configuring SOHO routers?

IP Addressing and Routing

35:    What are the metrics considered in Routing goals?

36:    Explain Static versus Dynamic Routing.

37:    Describe the routing process on the router from the point a packet enters one interface till it exits from another one.

38:    Which of the below are class B network addresses?

39:    What are the default IP address classes? What are their ranges?

40: What is a routing protocol?

41: Describe "classless" addressing.

42: A router received a packet on one of its interfaces. It searched its routing table for a match and found a route pointing out of its Fast Ethernet interface into another router. Which protocol will the router use to know the address that will be placed in the layer2 frame?

43: Describe IP routing protocols mentioning three functions of them.

44: This IP address 143.111.232.022 belongs to which address class?

45: Write the network address of this IP address 193.123.112.023 and also identify its class.

46: What are the steps involved in computing 'Address Assignment'?

47: How address is dynamically assigned to host?

TCP/IP Applications

48: Explain the following:

49: Explain UDP.

50: Which protocol below allows network hosts to resolve network IPs of other hosts knowing their hostnames?

51: What is TCP Error Recovery?

52: Which of the below are functions of TCP protocol?

53: Which of the below protocols use TCP as their transport protocol?

54: Describe TCP connection establishment and termination processes.

55: Why UDP is suitable for VOIP traffic?

Network Security

56: Explain ARP and RARP.

57: What is SSO?

58: What is the DoS attack?

59: What is Spyware?

60: What are Firewalls and what is their function?

61: Describe the DMZ network zone highlighting its functionality.

LAN Switching Concepts

62: What are HUB, Switch, and Router?

63: How does the switch understand the MAC address?

64: Which field in the frame does the switch use to deliver the frame to its destination?

65: Describe the process of building the switch's MAC address table.

66: The frames of the set of LAN interfaces collide with each other, however not with frames sent by any other devices in the network is called

67: What is STP?

68: How do you define a VLAN?

69: What is the maximum segment length of Ethernet CAT5 UTP cable?

Cisco LAN Switches Operation and Configuration

70: Which cable type do you use to access the console of Cisco switch?

71: You want to save the router configuration. Which command do you use to accomplish that?

72: Why is it recommended to use SSH instead of telnet in accessing Cisco devices?

73: You want to configure Telnet password of "cisco" for Cisco switch. Which command below do you use?

74: In which mode can the network administrator configure enable password for the router?

75: How do you reach the global configuration mode of Cisco switch remotely using your PC?

76: To reach enable mode from a vty (Telnet or SSH), the switch must be configured with:

77: How do you enable SSH access to the router?

78: Which command do you use to configure a gateway of 10.10.10.1 for a switch?

79: What is "port security"?

80: Which command do you use to configure a new VLAN on a switch?

81: How do you view the configured VLANs on a switch?

82: What is CDP?

83: You issued a "shutdown" command under one interface of a switch. Which of the below is the correct status of the interface?

84: How do you view the stored MAC addresses on a switch?

Wireless LAN Concepts

85: Describe WLAN Infrastructure mode.

86: Which of the below are security standards used in WLANs?

87: What is the maximum speed of 802.11a WLAN standard?

88: Which of the below is a private class B IP address?

IP Addressing and Subnetting

89: What is a private IP address?

90: If the subnet mask 255.255.255.192 is used with a class C network, how many subnets and how many users per subnet could exist?

91: What is the broadcast IP address of the network 192.168.14.32/28?

92: You have a class C network that you will use inside your network. What subnet mask can you use to get at least 6 subnets with 5 users in each one? Your design should allow for maximum number of subnets for future expansion.

93: Which of the below IP addresses are in the same subnet with the IP address 190.22.34.123 with mask 255.255.255.0?

94: Which address does the router use to forward the traffic?

Cisco Routers Operation and Configuration

95: What are Cisco SOHO routers?

96: Which cable type do you use to connect a router to a switch?

97: You want to view all IP addresses that are configured on all interfaces of a Cisco router. Which command below will you use?

98: How do you troubleshoot an interface with "administratively down -down" status?

99: What command below will you use to configure the ip address 10.10.10.10/24 on a router interface?

Routing Protocols Concepts and Troubleshooting

100: What is the route metric?

101: A router has two routes with different metrics. How will the router deal with them?

102: What is the RIP metric?

103: Which parameters does EIGRP use to calculate its metric?

104: Which routing protocols below support VLSM?

105: A router has two routes to the same destination; one learned by OSPF and the other learned by EIGRP. Which route will be used and why?

106: What is the function of ARP protocol?

107: You want to display detailed network configuration on Windows based host. This should include all interfaces, including IP address, mask, default gateway, and DNS IP addresses. Which command below should you use?

108: What command do you use on Cisco router to view the routing table?

109: What are the steps needed to enable telnet access to a router?

110: Which command below will check reachability between two end points by listing the IP addresses of the routers in the route?

111: What is a routed protocol?

112: Which of the below is a routed protocol?

113: Which of the below are routing protocols?

114: What is an IGP?

115: What is the metric used in distance vector routing protocols?

116: Which routing protocol below is a hybrid routing protocol?

117: What is routing convergence?

118: Which routing protocol below doesn't send subnet mask in the routing updates?

119: Which routing protocol below supports unequal-cost load balancing?

120: What is the administrative distance of OSPF?

121: What is Route poisoning?

122: Describe Split Horizon.

123: Compare Link State routing protocols to Distance Vector routing protocols.

124: Which routing protocol uses the link state logic?

125: You issued "show ip route" command on a Cisco router. Which letter below will appear in the start of the EIGRP learned route?

126: What does the "passive-interface" command do in EIGRP?

127: Which command below would you use to show only OSPF learned routes in the routing table?

128: In troubleshooting OSPF problems, which command can you use to show the neighbor of OSPF enabled router?

129: What is the 'routing protocol' and 'routed protocol'?

130: What is the purpose of a metric?

131: Name some routing protocols and routed protocols.

132: Describe about IP routing.

133: How Distance vector protocol differs from link state vector protocol?

134: In the given diagram which routing path will be taken by using RIPv1 and why?

135: List Classless and Classfull routing protocol.

136: Identify the metric used by distance vector protocol.

137: What are the disadvantages of proxy ARP?

138: What is ARP spoofing?

139: In which MAC method of sharing there is no collision?

140: Describe about FTP and TFTP protocols.

141: How will you set the bandwidth usage of EIGRP?

142: What is the formula to compute the waiting time of the queued packet before transmitting?

143: Which is routing protocol is best for smaller IP based network?

144: What are the limitations of RIP v1?

145: What are the features of RIPv2?

146: What are the limitations of RIPv2?

147: Which protocol is used as Interior Gateway Protocol?

148: What are the disadvantages of OSPF?

149: Give an example of OSPF.

150: Describe Type 1 and Type 2 of link state advertisement.

151: Describe about Type 3 and Type 4 of link state advertisement.

152: Which type of LSA is used to provide links that are external to the autonomous system?

Ethernet Virtual LANs (VLAN)

153: Which of the below is equivalent to a VLAN?

154: List at least two benefits of creating VLANs.

155: What is a trunk?

156: Which of the below are valid VTP modes?

157: Which command below can you use to configure VLAN "20" in a switch?

158: Which command do you use to assign a switch port in VLAN "5"?

159: Which command do you use to set the switch port mode to trunk?

Spanning-Tree Protocol

160: How spanning tree Root Bridge is elected in layer 2 networks?

161: Which of the below are valid IEEE 802.1d Spanning-Tree protocol port states?

162: What is the benefit of Etherchannel?

163: What is the function of spanning-tree Portfast?

164: Which STP port role do ports of the root bridge use?

165: You want to change spanning-tree Bridge ID value on a Cisco switch, which command below will you use to do that?

Troubleshooting LAN Switching

166: You want to disable CDP on a specific switch. Which command do you use?

167: A switch port is in the "down down" status. Which of the below are possible problems in that interface?

168: You want to view the MAC addresses learned by the switch. Which command do you use?

169: What is DHCP?

170: Describe the function of ICMP.

171: Which of the below trunking protocols support native VLAN?

172: Which trunking protocol below encapsulates the Ethernet frame into a new layer 2 header and trailer?

Static Routing

173: What does the character "S" means in the routing table?

174: Which route is preferred by a router, a Static route or OSPF learned route? Why?

175: What is the default Maximum Transmission Unit (MTU) of Ethernet interface?

VLSM and Route Summarization

176: What is VLSM and what does it mean in the networking terminology?

177: Which routing protocols below support VLSM?

178: Which subnet mask would you use over point-to-point WAN links and why?

179: What is route summarization and what are the benefits of it?

180: What is the broadcast address of the subnet 183.15.32.0/20?

181: Which routing protocols below support Manual route summarization?

Control Network Traffic with Access Control Lists (ACLs)

182: What is the function of IP Access Control List (ACL)?

183: Where is the recommended ACL application point in the network for ACLs?

184: What is the benefit of Extended ACL over Standard ACL?

185: Which of the below can be used as matching criteria in Extended ACL?

OSPF Concepts

186: Which OSPF multicast address do routers send hello packet to?

187: To form neighbor relationship in OSPF, two routers must agree on some parameters. Which of the below must match before two routers

188: What is OSPF "Hello Interval"?

189: How do you define OSPF ABR router?

190: What is OSPF Inter-area route?

191: You want to statically configure OSPF router ID. Which command below will you use?

192: Which of the below is used to calculate OSPF route cost?

193: OSPF authentication is an important feature to secure OSPF domain. What authentication types are supported by OSPF?

194: By default, how many OSPF equal-cost routes can be inserted in the routing table for load balancing?

EIGRP Concepts

195: In order for EIGRP neighbor relationship to form, which of the below must be validated?

196: List at least three characteristics of PPP.

197: Which of the below is used by default in EIGRP metric calculation?

198: What is EIGRP feasible distance?

199: What is the feasible successor route in EIGRP?

200: Which of the below algorithms is used by EIGRP to recover a failed route with no feasible successor?

201: How do you define a new EIGRP process on a router with AS 1?

202: Which authentication types below are supported by EIGRP?

203: What types of load balancing does EIGRP support?

Point-to-Point WAN Links and Protocols

204: At which OSI reference model layer does PPP operate?

205: Which of the below are functions of PPP LCP?

206: Which of the below are PPP authentication types?

207: What is the function of PPP multilink?

208: What is the function of the "Protocol" field in PPP?

Frame-Relay Configuration and Troubleshooting

209: What is Frame-relay?

210: What is Frame Relay LMI protocol?

211: What is the function of DLCI in Frame-relay?

212: How does frame-relay deal with broadcast?

213: What is the FECN bit in Frame Relay and what does it mean to set it to 1?

214: What is DE bit of frame-relay header and when it is set?

215: Which of the below are valid frame-relay LMI types?

216: Which of the below are valid frame-relay encapsulation types?

217: What command do you use to select the interface encapsulation as frame-relay?

218: Which command below will you use to set an address for frame-relay virtual circuit?

219: What is the function of Inverse ARP?

Virtual Private Networks (VPN)

220: Which of the below are valid VPN types?

221: Virtual Private Networks (VPN) provide data integrity. What is data integrity?

222: Which of the below are benefits of Virtual Private Networks (VPN)?

223: Which of the below are valid VPN encryption algorithms?

224: How do VPNs achieve data privacy?

Network Address Translation (NAT)

225: What are the benefits of using Network Address Translation (NAT)?

226: Which of the below are private IP address?

227: In NAT terminology, what does the term Inside Global mean?

228: What is PAT?

229: Which command do you use to clear the dynamic entries in the router's NAT table?

IP Version 6 (IPv6)

230: What are the advantages of using IPv6?

231: What is IPv6 Anycast IP address?

232: Select the shortest valid abbreviation for the IPv6 address

233: Which of the below are IPv6 routing protocols?

234: What is IPv6 EUI-64 address format?

Subnet Masking

235: How will you compute network and host part of the given IP address say 192.194.211.078?

236: What does it mean when network address is all 0's or 1's?

237: What is called classless Inter Domain Routing?

238: Calculate the number of host and subnets for the given IP address (158.220.78.24) with subnet mask of 7 bits.

239: What is the use of CIDR?

Networks and Protocols

240: What is converged network?

241: Explain session layer with a real time example.

242: What is a port?

243: For the following services provide their corresponding protocols:

244: What is the use of "show ipx servers" command?

245: Describe about communication protocol.

246: Is it wise to set a single protocol to handle all data communication? If not, what action is to be taken to solve this problem?

247: What is Fault tolerance?

248: Describe the two authentication protocols in PPP.

249: What is P2P network and their application?

250: What are the types of record stored in DNS?

251: In case of sharing large messages which process is employed?

252: How is Corruption of data prevented?

253: Point the difference between VTY and AYT.

254: What is the use of netsat?

255: What is the purpose of setting the TTL value?

256: What is SMB?

257: Why IPV4 network is also referred as broadcast domain?

258: What are the early versions of the Ethernet?

259: What is the advantage of the switch over a hub in Ethernet?

260: What is goodput?

Cisco IOS

261: What is 'user EXEC level'?

262: When a user can get into the privileged EXEC level?

263: Describe about 'Global' and 'Interface' configuration mode.

HR Interview Questions

1: Where do you find ideas?

2: How do you achieve creativity in the workplace?

3: How do you push others to create ideas?

4: Describe your creativity.

5: How would you handle a negative coworker?

6: What would you do if you witnessed a coworker surfing the web, reading a book, etc, wasting company time?

7: How do you handle competition among yourself and other employees?

8: When is it okay to socialize with coworkers?

9: Tell me about a time when a major change was made at your last job, and how you handled it.

10: When delegating tasks, how do you choose which tasks go to which team members?

11: Tell me about a time when you had to stand up for something you believed strongly about to coworkers or a supervisor.

12: Tell me about a time when you helped someone finish their work, even though it wasn't "your job."

13: What are the challenges of working on a team? How do you handle this?

14: Do you value diversity in the workplace?

15: How would you handle a situation in which a coworker was not accepting of someone else's diversity?

16: Are you rewarded more from working on a team, or accomplishing a task on your own?

17: Tell me about a time when you didn't meet a deadline.

18: How do you eliminate distractions while working?

19: Tell me about a time when you worked in a position with a weekly or monthly quota to meet. How often were you successful?

20: Tell me about a time when you met a tough deadline, and how you were able to complete it.

21: How do you stay organized when you have multiple projects on your plate?

50: What type of worker are you?

51: Tell me about your happiest day at work.

52: Tell me about your worst day at work.

53: What are you passionate about?

54: What is the piece of criticism you receive most often?

55: What type of work environment do you succeed the most in?

56: Are you an emotional person?

57: Ten years ago, what were your career goals?

58: Tell me about a weakness you used to have, and how you changed it.

59: Tell me about your goal-setting process.

60: Tell me about a time when you solved a problem by creating actionable steps to follow.

61: Where do you see yourself five years from now?

62: When in a position, do you look for opportunities to promote?

63: On a scale of 1 to 10, how successful has your life been?

64: What is your greatest goal in life?

65: Tell me about a time when you set a goal in your personal life and achieved it.

66: What is your greatest goal in your career?

67: Tell me about a time when you achieved a goal.

68: What areas of your work would you still like to improve in? What are your plans to do this?

69: What is customer service?

70: Tell me about a time when you went out of your way for a customer.

71: How do you gain confidence from customers?

72: Tell me about a time when a customer was upset or agitated – how did you handle the situation?

73: When can you make an exception for a customer?

74: What would you do in a situation where you were needed by both a customer and your boss?

75: What is the most important aspect of customer service?

76: Is it best to create low or high expectations for a customer?

Some of the following titles might also be handy:

1. NET Interview Questions You'll Most Likely Be Asked
2. Access VBA Programming Interview Questions You'll Most Likely Be Asked
3. Adobe ColdFusion Interview Questions You'll Most Likely Be Asked
4. Advanced C++ Interview Questions You'll Most Likely Be Asked
5. Advanced Excel Interview Questions You'll Most Likely Be Asked
6. Advanced JAVA Interview Questions You'll Most Likely Be Asked
7. Advanced SAS Interview Questions You'll Most Likely Be Asked
8. AJAX Interview Questions You'll Most Likely Be Asked
9. Algorithms Interview Questions You'll Most Likely Be Asked
10. Android Development Interview Questions You'll Most Likely Be Asked
11. Ant & Maven Interview Questions You'll Most Likely Be Asked
12. Apache Web Server Interview Questions You'll Most Likely Be Asked
13. Artificial Intelligence Interview Questions You'll Most Likely Be Asked
14. ASP.NET Interview Questions You'll Most Likely Be Asked
15. Automated Software Testing Interview Questions You'll Most Likely Be Asked
16. Base SAS Interview Questions You'll Most Likely Be Asked
17. BEA WebLogic Server Interview Questions You'll Most Likely Be Asked
18. C & C++ Interview Questions You'll Most Likely Be Asked
19. C# Interview Questions You'll Most Likely Be Asked
20. CCNA Interview Questions You'll Most Likely Be Asked
21. Cloud Computing Interview Questions You'll Most Likely Be Asked
22. Computer Architecture Interview Questions You'll Most Likely Be Asked
23. Computer Networks Interview Questions You'll Most Likely Be Asked
24. Core JAVA Interview Questions You'll Most Likely Be Asked
25. Data Structures & Algorithms Interview Questions You'll Most Likely Be Asked
26. EJB 3.0 Interview Questions You'll Most Likely Be Asked
27. Entity Framework Interview Questions You'll Most Likely Be Asked
28. Fedora & RHEL Interview Questions You'll Most Likely Be Asked
29. Hadoop BIG DATA Interview Questions You'll Most Likely Be Asked
30. Hibernate, Spring & Struts Interview Questions You'll Most Likely Be Asked
31. HR Interview Questions You'll Most Likely Be Asked
32. HTML, XHTML and CSS Interview Questions You'll Most Likely Be Asked
33. HTML5 Interview Questions You'll Most Likely Be Asked
34. IBM WebSphere Application Server Interview Questions You'll Most Likely Be Asked
35. iOS SDK Interview Questions You'll Most Likely Be Asked
36. Java / J2EE Design Patterns Interview Questions You'll Most Likely Be Asked
37. Java / J2EE Interview Questions You'll Most Likely Be Asked
38. JavaScript Interview Questions You'll Most Likely Be Asked
39. JavaServer Faces Interview Questions You'll Most Likely Be Asked
40. JDBC Interview Questions You'll Most Likely Be Asked
41. jQuery Interview Questions You'll Most Likely Be Asked
42. JSP-Servlet Interview Questions You'll Most Likely Be Asked
43. JUnit Interview Questions You'll Most Likely Be Asked
44. Linux Interview Questions You'll Most Likely Be Asked
45. Linux System Administrator Interview Questions You'll Most Likely Be Asked
46. Mac OS X Lion Interview Questions You'll Most Likely Be Asked
47. Mac OS X Snow Leopard Interview Questions You'll Most Likely Be Asked
48. Microsoft Access Interview Questions You'll Most Likely Be Asked
49. Microsoft Powerpoint Interview Questions You'll Most Likely Be Asked
50. Microsoft Word Interview Questions You'll Most Likely Be Asked

51. MySQL Interview Questions You'll Most Likely Be Asked
52. Networking Interview Questions You'll Most Likely Be Asked
53. OOPS Interview Questions You'll Most Likely Be Asked
54. Operating Systems Interview Questions You'll Most Likely Be Asked
55. Oracle Database Administration Interview Questions You'll Most Likely Be Asked
56. Oracle E-Business Suite Interview Questions You'll Most Likely Be Asked
57. ORACLE PL/SQL Interview Questions You'll Most Likely Be Asked
58. Perl Programming Interview Questions You'll Most Likely Be Asked
59. PHP Interview Questions You'll Most Likely Be Asked
60. Python Interview Questions You'll Most Likely Be Asked
61. RESTful JAVA Web Services Interview Questions You'll Most Likely Be Asked
62. SAP HANA Interview Questions You'll Most Likely Be Asked
63. SAS Programming Guidelines Interview Questions You'll Most Likely Be Asked
64. Selenium Testing Tools Interview Questions You'll Most Likely Be Asked
65. Silverlight Interview Questions You'll Most Likely Be Asked
66. Software Repositories Interview Questions You'll Most Likely Be Asked
67. Software Testing Interview Questions You'll Most Likely Be Asked
68. SQL Server Interview Questions You'll Most Likely Be Asked
69. Tomcat Interview Questions You'll Most Likely Be Asked
70. UML Interview Questions You'll Most Likely Be Asked
71. Unix Interview Questions You'll Most Likely Be Asked
72. UNIX Shell Programming Interview Questions You'll Most Likely Be Asked
73. Windows Server 2008 R2 Interview Questions You'll Most Likely Be Asked
74. XLXP, XSLT, XPATH, XFORMS & XQuery Interview Questions You'll Most Likely Be Asked
75. XML Interview Questions You'll Most Likely Be Asked

For complete list visit

www.vibrantpublishers.com

Made in the USA
Las Vegas, NV
28 January 2024

85011478R00098